RISING TO THE TOP

INSIGHT PUBLISHING
SEVIERVILLE, TENNESSEE

Lindsay,

You are a superstar. I think you have huge potential and I want to make sure you achive all your dreams.

Best of luck

Rising To The Top

© 2006 by Insight Publishing Company.

Disclaimer: This book is a compilation of ideas from numerous experts who have each contributed a chapter. As such, the views expressed in each chapter are of those who were interviewed and not necessarily of the interviewer or Insight Publishing.

Published by Insight Publishing Company
647 Wall Street
Sevierville, TN 37862

Cover design: Emmy Shubert
Edited by: Sandra Pinkoski

10 9 8 7 6 5 4 3 2

Printed in the United States of America

ISBN: 1-60013- 074-7

Table of Contents

A Message from the Publisher

The finest and best rise to the top. Like cream in milk, people who excel in what they do rise head and shoulders above others in a crowd. How do they do it? Are they born with some driving force that pushes them along? Do they just suddenly decide they're going to do what it takes to rise above or do they just suddenly find themselves there?

I really wanted to find the answers to those questions so I looked for some outstanding people who would tell me what rising to the top means to them and how they rose to the top. I believe I found some folks who gave me some remarkable insights into how they did it. What they told me altered my perception of what rising to the top means—how it's done, why it's done, and most interesting of all, who is able to do it.

You will really be fascinated with what these authors have to say and I think the concepts they present will stretch your mind and give you a unique learning experience. You will have the facts you need to make important decisions about your rise to the top. Yes, it's possible for you to get there and sometimes it just takes that extra boost, that extra bit of knowledge to fill in the gaps. This book is not for those who are satisfied with mediocrity. It is for those of you who really want to know how you can "rise to the top."

Interviews conducted by:
David E. Wright
President, International Speakers Network

A Life By Design . . . Not By Accident!

Bonnie Dean

Rising to the top! What a concept—why doesn't everyone rise to the top? What separates those who have a life by design from those who rise to a level of mediocrity? Several experts contributed to this book. The beauty of our diversity of thinking is that you will be getting a number of varied opinions of what "rising to the top" means. Some of these chapters will resonate with your spirit and soul. Some may come back to haunt you at a later date. A wise man once said that people don't need to be taught, they just need to be reminded. Enjoy the journey through these pages of tips, tools, and reminders of ways to rise above the crowd and transform the ordinary into the extraordinary!

> *"A strong woman knows she has strength enough for the journey,*
> *but a woman of strength knows*
> *it is in the journey where she will become strong."*
> —Unknown

In Beijing China, in the middle of the Forbidden City there is a stone—a large stone. It is called the wishing stone. For thousands of years, Chinese Emperors have taken their place on the stone and wished for better crops, for success on the battlefield, for good health, and for many sons.

Now allowed in the Forbidden City, tourists take turns getting their pictures taken standing on the stone—closing their eyes and wishing for better health, riches, more in their relationships, more in their lives.

"Let others lead small lives, but not you.
Let others argue over small things, but not you.
Let others cry over small hurts, but not you.
Let others leave their future in someone else's hands,
but not you."

—Jim Rohn

What a powerful statement! Words well spoken can move us to action faster than wishing and hoping for things to change in our lives. My association with Jim Rohn began in 1981 and has produced dramatic results in my life more times than any wishing stone ever will. His mentorship has resulted in my speaking and coaching career taking me to several countries around the world. Jim's words have had trickle-down value into every area of the life of my business and the business of my life.

Back in the '70s, I made my living taking people backpacking for college credit on the island of Kauai and directing a summer sports-camp on the island for "over privileged" youth. In the off-season, I lived in San Diego training for marathons, teaching aerobics, and promoting the Hawaii programs. Life was good until I was diagnosed with skin cancer and went through a divorce, almost simultaneously.

People talk about events or circumstances that irrevocably change their lives. Hearing Jim Rohn speak for the first time was such a moment in mine. Two good friends took me to see Jim Rohn for the first time in early 1981. The copious notes I took that evening of Jim Rohn basics started me on a journey of self-development that continues today.

Whenever I stray from the path of positive personal development and take a seat at a pity party or at a self-doubt event, I refocus on the many Rohnisms that have helped shape the life I live today. I think of these sayings as Jim Rohn basics. They propelled me from a five-dollar-an-hour job in an attorney's office to a nonstop, knock-the-ball-out-of-the-park career in strictly commissioned sales.

They continue to give me the courage to take control and assume full responsibility for the outcomes of my actions. Jim Rohn provoked me to think and constantly re-evaluate having *A Life By Design . . . Not By Accident!*

Here are some of my favorite Rohnisms:

- "The view of the future is an awesome force. Are you in awe of your future?"
- "You better have a plan for your life or you are going to fall into someone else's plan."
- "Without dreams and visions we perish."
- "For things to change in your life—you must change!"
- "Reasons make the difference. When you have the why, the how will follow."
- "When you go to work on your goals. Your goals go to work on you!"
- "A casual approach to life will get you casual results."
- People don't plan to fail, they simply fail to plan."
- "You have to work harder on yourself than you do on your job."
- "Income seldom exceeds personal development."
- "Pay yourself first. Give 10 percent to those less fortunate."
- "Learn how to be happy with what you have while you pursue what you want."
- "Find out what poor people read and don't read it."
- "Keep the weeds out of your garden."
- "Learn from the negatives as well as the positives—what was the lesson learned?"
- The most important question isn't "What am I getting?" The most important question is "What am I becoming?"

There will be lots of quotes from others that I have considered mentors sprinkled throughout this chapter. These quotes have guided me through times of uncertainty and change.

> *"The secret of success is consistency of purpose"*
> —Benjamin Disraeli (1804–1881)

Life by Design . . . Not by Accident

> *"All difficult things have their origin in that which is easy, and great things in that which is small."*
> —Lao Tzu

In life, what you focus on tends to expand. A major lesson gleaned in the early '80s was to focus on where I wanted to be spiritually, mentally, financially, physically, and socially that year, in three years, in five years, in ten years.

To sharpen that focus, writing down those goals in a journal and reviewing them regularly began the process of personal self-development. It's like a visual contract you make with yourself. It shows that you are a serious student of your own life! The next step to *A Life by Design* is to break down each of the goals in bite-sized pieces. It became my *"a little a lot"* theory: You just focus on doing the little things well. Just do a little each day and *a little a lot* becomes more. Then you look back after a few months or a whole year and you will find so many new skills you have acquired, relationships deepened, books read, miles ran, money saved, places visited, and memories created. It reminds me of the hokey pokey: When you put your right arm in—that is a little. When you put your left arm in—that's a little more. When you put your whole self in, *a little a lot* has become much more! A life by design is all about putting your whole self in to the life of your business and most importantly, the business of your life! *"That's what it's all about!"*

A perfect example of doing *a little a lot* hits me every spring when I'm fighting for time to work in my yard. When my husband retired, we pulled up our Southern California roots and moved out of the city into the Pacific Northwest woods. We bought a one-hundred-year-old craftsman home and settled onto two wooded acres above a thirteen-mile-long lake. When other family members viewed "Big Trees" for the first time, with our one hundred-plus-year-old firs and cedars, eight large flower beds, park-sized expanse of lawn, and overabundance of maintenance work they blurted out, "What were you thinking?"

My husband, "Saint" David and I, are in hog heaven. We are at the center of the family hub. The old country kitchen and massive dining room, inviting guest rooms, and worthy of *National Geographic* wildlife have made our home a gathering place for friends and family. It doesn't hurt that Andra, the oldest daughter, is a gourmet cook!

We have opened our doors to non-profit and service groups for board retreats and planning sessions on numerous occasions. There is no better place in the world to come home to after a week of being a road warrior than to Big Trees. A huge old porch wraps around two sides of the house with rocking chairs inviting one sit and gaze at the lake. Yet, when spring arrives and the dandelions start popping their golden blooms in all of my flowerbeds and throughout the lawn I wonder how we'll ever stay on top of it. (Of course you can relate this to other kinds of "weeds" you get in the lives of your business and the business of your life.)

My office is located on our property above our garage. I take several mental breaks during the course of a regular workday. While walking the three dogs (two sassy pugs and Charlie "The Wonder Dog"), I have made it a personal goal to pull one hundred weeds a walk. I carry a bag and a tool. I generally walk the dogs four times a day—that's four hundred weeds a day I am obliterating. Picture five days a week at four hundred little weeding walks and you grasp the concept of two thousand wicked little weeds on their way to the green waste dump. That's doing a little a lot, and it adds up exponentially. To think about pulling up two thousand weeds is overwhelming. I can get my gloves around a mere hundred at a pop. Looking back at the progress made in clearing flower beds over the last six months, I am amazed at the job a bite-sized goal each day can accomplish.

Now refocus on a little not being done daily. In no time at all little things can become a big problem.

- Not making those phone calls
- Not following up on leads
- Not getting in that workout
- Not reading that book or listening to that CD
- Not communicating with the people we love
- Not taking time to take care of ourselves

Doing *a little a lot* every day to keep the weeds at bay is like putting daily deposits in your emotional, physical, mental, social, financial bank accounts compound with interest and *a little a lot* becomes *more!*

> *"The man who removes a mountain begins*
> *by carrying away small stones."*
> —Chinese Proverb

For over fifteen years I have been sharing the belief that we live in a high tech/low tech society—a hungry society hungry for a personal touch, a listening ear. Most of the unease, unrest, dissatisfaction, disease, and unhappiness in our world today is caused by people living *below* their capacity.

Self-Mastery

"The tragedy in life is not that we aimed too high
and did not reach our goal.
The tragedy in life is that we aim too low and reach it."
—Michelangelo

What most determines success in life on this God-given planet of possibilities that we all share? According to a Carnegie Foundation study, a mere 15 percent of success in life is based on technical skills. That makes sense. You wouldn't want a surgeon to operate on you without having technical skills. The intriguing statistic the study revealed was that 85 percent of success in life is based on our ability to communicate with others and our ability to manage ourselves. (It is important to note here it didn't say our ability to manage others!)

"Mastering others is strength.
Mastering yourself is true power."
—Lao Tzu

How do we go about mastering ourselves to unleash the true power for *a life by design . . . not by accident?* One tool is to have a work/life balance game plan that reflects your deepest values, commitments, and heart's longings, to review it often, and have a positive support team to encourage you on and celebrate your successes with you!

Twice Jim Rohn has altered the course of my life. The first time, after hearing Jim I entered a career in direct sales. By applying the principles I learned, I remained in the top 10 percent throughout. Rising to the top during these years included navigating through the rough waters of moving three times in two years, our family being abandoned by our father, a new marriage, and being audited by the IRS—and that's just the tip of the iceberg. Creating my own sunny weather and maintaining a positive attitude made the difference between being a victim or working on that life by design. A decade after I attended Jim's seminar I was fortunate enough to have the opportunity to work with Jim as a promoter of his seminars in Southern California. I would put an average of fifty to one hundred fifty miles a day on my car, five days a week, as a guest speaker at various real estate and insurance offices, financial institutes, direct sales, and MLM meetings.

At these meetings I would share Jim's philosophy of life and sell tickets to his upcoming programs in Los Angeles and Orange County. These were sixteen of the most memorable months of my life. I couldn't believe I got paid to be a part of Achievement Seminars International.

In January 1993, I joined the National Speakers Association and started my own company, W.O.W. Presentations. W.O.W. stood for What Others Want, which I believe is H.O.P.E. I built my speaking/coaching business on the premise that we all desperately want to make a difference and we can do so by:

H—helping
O—other
P—people
E—every day to expect more from themselves.

Fourteen years later the acronym W.O.W. was changed and now stands for Wise Older Woman. Focusing on the foundation of my association with the master of motivation (Jim Rohn), I have had the good fortune to travel the world speaking about creating core connections and staying in touch with what really matters. For over twenty-five years I have personally worked *a little a lot* at creating *a life by design . . . not by accident.*

> *"If we can just stretch and improve 1 percent each day,*
> *the positive effects will reverberate*
> *through every aspect of our lives."*
> —Bonnie Dean

Six Branches of Your Life That Create Balance

> *"We are what we repeatedly do.*
> *Excellence, then, is not an act but a habit."*
> —Aristotle

To create and live *a life by design* there needs to be a plan in place. My husband is a private pilot. We had a Cessna 182 for sixteen years that we flew all over the West Coast of the United States and Canada. We would never consider taking off without a flight plan. Due to sudden weather shifts, on several trips our flight plan needed to be altered, often more than once. Flexibility became a mainstay of our flights. *Blessed are the flexible for they will not be bent out of shape.*

A chef would never make a cake without a recipe—why would our own lives seem any less important? We should have a plan in place to guide us. Think of your game plan as a tree. There are six main branches on the tree of work/life balance. They grow at different rates as they are trimmed and nurtured by the way we handle the events in our lives. If one side becomes too heavy the tree will break. We see this illustrated in the divorce rate in our country and in the percent of adults and children who are obese, unhappy, and unfulfilled.

Let's look at the six branches and explore ways to keep them growing strong and reaching up to the sun—rising to the top.

The Spiritual Branch:

This is an important area to examine. If you don't stand for something it's easy to fall for anything.

I grew up though YMCA summer camps and service club programs. I own the spirit, mind, and body philosophy at a cellular level. Yet, when my speaking business took off, I let this branch of my tree wither and fall way. If my family could fit into my busy schedule back then . . . good for them. I started to believe my own press clips and I wrote them! At times, it got pretty lonely feeling like I was "out there" doing it all on my own. It took a tragic incident like the 1995 Oklahoma City bombing to bring me back to my senses. Seeing that fireman walk out of the building with the limp child in his arms and sensing that many people were going to have regrets about words unspoken to those they lost that day forced me to once again refocus on what truly matters in life.

I invited God back as the foundation in my life, my family second, and my career third. With my life values at the top of my list the speaking and coaching came easier. My life began to flow freely again with the foundation of that focus on the roots of my tree. Funny, back in 1993 I had given each of my Life Mastery Seminar participants a small tree seedling to tend to as they nurtured their own work/life balance—to watch it grow as they grew and designed their own lives. How easy it is to get out of focus and lose sight of what really matters.

Too often I'm reminded that I teach what I most need to learn!

Explore the mysteries of whatever this branch means to you and find a foundation that gives you inner strength and peace of mind.

*"Belief consists in accepting the affirmations of the soul;
unbelief, in denying them."*
—Ralph Waldo Emerson

The Family Branch:

The next branch represents your family. Success at the expense of family and friends looks more like failure than success.

When I interview audience members prior to my preparing a presentation for them, I often ask them why they work such long hours. Usually, the first three or four answers I get as I dig deeper into the root of the question are not the real answers. Finally, most respond that they work long hours to "make a better life for my family." Interestingly, what usually gets put on the back burner in our fast-paced workaholic society today is the *family!* With both parents working in more than 70 percent of the households today we come home tired and spent and just want to sit down and relax. The kids are excited to show Mom and Dad what they did at school. We tend to put them off to get through the evening's chores. Instead of building self-worth in each other everyone feels undervalued and unimportant.

Practice the "magic of a minute and a half" to fertilize your family branch. When someone needs your attention, pause and give him or her ninety seconds of it—undivided, with direct eye and heart contact. You will be amazed at what that minute and a half delivers. A hug and comments on what your child or your spouse had to share sends him or her away feeling valued and genuinely listened to, and the branch thrives. All it takes, honestly, is 90 seconds! Try it. You will be surprised at the immediate results!

When you are working long hours on a project that takes you away from your family, put a chart up on the refrigerator. Let the family put stars on the chart each time you have to leave them. Involve them in the goal. Five stars equals a movie night, twenty stars means a weekend get-away. Now the family is part of the process and they feel valued.

"Dad, may I help you carry your briefcase to the car?" They are now involved in the outcomes!

Do you have children you want to send to college someday? Is there a plan in place or are you closing your eyes and crossing your fingers and wishing for it to happen? Consider creating a "family dream board" where you tape pictures of places you plan to go, things you want for your home, activities you plan on participating in, and goals for the family. A new board is created each year as the old one is retired and takes its place in the family memory books.

Remember the words to the Crosby, Stills, and Nash song: "Teach Your Children Well."

> *"The only real control we have is how we respond*
> *to the stress in our day-to-day lives."*
>
> —Bonnie Dean

The Financial Branch:

Make financial independence a main goal and value in your life. According to a recent Gallup poll, most marriages that run into trouble are in jeopardy because of mishandled money matters. *The Richest man in Babylon* by George Clason can be an insightful tool for getting on track financially. Use credit cards to establish credit but only charge what you can pay off monthly—no exceptions. Remember, as a child, half the fun of getting something was the anticipation! Keep this branch strong and it will be a source of strength for your entire tree.

> *"If your outgo exceeds your income,*
> *your upkeep will be your downfall."*
>
> —Bill Morgan

The Social Branch:

Who do you invest your time with? There are two kinds of people on this planet. There are mentors and tormentors. People are either a positive influence in our lives, helping us reach the stars or are slowly, for whatever reason, knocking us off course. Tormentors sometimes come disguised as family members or so-called friends.

Spend your time with people who challenge you to be all that you can be. Don't shy away from those who hold you accountable. Cherish those who hold your feet to the fire and those who will accept no excuses for poor performance or bad behavior. My husband of over twenty years is my strongest supporter and my most honest critic. The friends I value most are those who call me on my sometimes poor behavior and still love me.

This is also the limb that flourishes with your involvement in charities and service clubs within your community. Cavett Robert, founder of the National Speakers Association, said, "You can never out-give yourself." The more you give back to those less fortunate, the more you appreciate what you have. Encourage people you know who feel that life has let them down to get involved in community service. There is a good chance their life focus might change as they help lift up others.

> *"What lies behind us and what lies before us are tiny matters compared to what lies within us."*
> —Ralph Waldo Emerson

The Mental Branch:

Two things that greatly affect our lives most are the people we meet and the books we read.

In the workbooks for all of my presentations, the last page is always a resource page of great books that relate to the topic. You can e-mail me at Bonnie@bonnedean.com and I will send you a list on leadership, stress-busters, self-development, team-building, health and wellness, sales, etc. Build an eclectic library. Read it all— biographies, fiction, non-fiction, history, religion, arts and science, geography, and political science. Books are such an excellent tool to learn, explore, stretch, and become more.

> *"Education is the best provision for the journey to old age."*
> —Aristotle

The Physical Branch:

> *"If you can't fly, then run. If you can't run, then walk. If you can't walk, then crawl. But whatever you do, keep moving."*
> —Dr. Martin Luther King, Jr.

Your health *is* your wealth. How can you possibly do well in any area of your life if you don't feel well? Thirty minutes a day is all it takes. Get rid of all the processed foods in your kitchen and start fueling your body with healthy fruits and vegetables. Drink lots of water and pass on the sodas. We all know what to do. Are we doing what we know? Stephen Covey, author of *The 7 Habits of Highly Effective People*, states, *"Just because something is common sense, doesn't mean it is common practice."* Jim Rohn taught me: *"Easy to do, easy not to do!"* The choice is yours. Prepare and prevent makes more sense than repair and repent.

Keep this branch strong and it will support you during lean times.

> *"Forget past mistakes. Forget failures.*
> *Forget everything except*
> *what you are going to do now and do it"*
> —William Durant
> Founder of General Motors

Charles Garfield, author of *Peak Performers,* sums up what we have covered so far:

"Searching for the peak performer within yourself has one basic meaning: You recognize yourself as a person who was born, not as a peak performer but as a learner. With the capacity to grow, change, and reach for the highest possibilities of human nature, you regard yourself as a person in process. Not perfect, but a person who keeps asking: What more can I be? What else can I achieve that will benefit me and my company? That will contribute to my family and my community?"

I couldn't have said it better myself. When I started my career in a direct sales company, earning strictly commissions on what I sold, well meaning friends and family thought I was on pretty shaky ground.

A decade later, when I left that career to promote Jim Rohn, those same people asked how I could leave my *secure* direct sales career for an unknown! I had learned that security was my own ability to produce results. I knew I could count on me!

When I designed my Sales Aerobics Seminars—a boot camp for people in commissioned sales careers—I revisited the concepts that propelled me into the top 10 percent and kept me there for over a decade. You see, success in any area of life is not an accident—it's a game plan of habits!

Below are the six habits that have guided me in building and revitalizing my road to success in life's journey:

Six Habits for Personal Success

1. Maintain a Positive Mental Attitude (PMA)

> *"I think what I represent is achieving what you want in life.*
> *It's a matter of your attitude.*
> *Some people have a negative attitude,*
> *and that's their disability."*
> —Marla Runyan, legally blind
> U.S. 1,500 meter Olympian

My father was my first success coach. I remember him coming in to wake us every morning declaring; "It's a beautiful day in Southern California. The birds are singing, the sun is shining. Get up sleepy heads—enjoy the day!" Funny thing was, he used the same greeting rain or shine. My father taught us to create our own weather pattern. You create your day, your week, your month, your year. That personal habit has carried me through some of life's toughest storms—an alcoholic parent, divorce, having a HIV positive family member, a sibling who has spent time in prison, a sister who spent time in a battered women's shelter with her kids, and more! I am convinced that the dysfunctional family is the norm. We all have stories. When I opened up and started sharing my stories with my audiences I began to better connect and share tools to help them choose the road to a PMA.

2. Ongoing Life Education

School is never out for the professional student of life.

Two things that will significantly alter your *rising to the top* are the books you read and the people you spend your time with. Be eager to stretch your mental muscles. Experts are saying that college age students today will have a minimum of seven careers and that five of those careers have not even been created yet! Invest in yourself and keep learning.

> *"The illiterate of the twenty-first century*
> *will not be those who cannot read and write,*
> *but those who cannot learn, unlearn, and relearn."*
> —Alvin Toffler
> American writer and futurist

Travel has gotten crazy since 9/11. To help ward off the stress of late flights and long hours at the airport I took up knitting. It's a new skill that has produced fabulous gifts for friends and reduced anxiety for me. I learned how to do it from a book.

3. Daily Commitment to Your Goals

"Excellence is not something attained and put in a trophy case.
It is not sought after, achieved, and, thereafter, a steady state.
It is a momentary phenomenon, a rare conjunction of
body, mind, and spirit at one's peak.
Should I come to that peak, I cannot stay there.
Like Sisyphus, I must start each day at the bottom
and work back up to the top.
And then beyond that peak to another and yet another."
—Dr. George Sheehan

This third habit really rang true for me when I started my speaking career. One of my mentors had cautioned me that it can take three to five years to build a speaking and coaching business. That helped me tremendously when I got discouraged and felt like giving up. I kept focusing on doing *a little a lot.* I would speak as often as I could for a low fee or no fee to get my name and my message out there. I networked like a crazy woman to meet people who I felt I could be of value to. It was constantly putting one foot in front of the other and believing in my heart that one day all the hard work and effort would pay off. Looking back over that last fifteen years, I can trace back major clients who connected with me in those first few years.

"Just keep swimming . . . just keep swimming . . .
just keep swimming."
—Dory the fish in *Finding Nemo*
(This "power-phrase" helps out
in situations well beyond the water.)

4. Willingness to Take Risks

"Life shrinks or expands in proportion to one's courage."
—Anais Nin

Life is full of risks. Two of the saddest words in the English language are "if only." Every time I have encountered a fork in the road and took the riskiest one, I grew the most. Sometimes the choice meant leaving friends, cities, states, my country, and my comfort zone behind. They weren't always the safest or the easiest choices to make. Life is about choice management. I have lived in three states, worked in several countries, been married to two wonderful men, been self-employed most of my life and placed myself in several life threatening situations. No regrets. I've never had children of my own, but have been a step-parent for almost twenty-five years. With risk comes reward. A lesson learned, a new skill acquired, a new sense of self-worth all are results of taking a risk.

"Twenty years from now you will be more disappointed
by the things you didn't do than by the ones you did do.
So throw off the bowlines.
Sail away from the safe harbor.
Catch the trade winds in your sales.
Explore. Dream. Discover."
—Mark Twain

5. PX5 Passion, Plan, Purpose, Patience, Persistence

"We are made to persist. That is how we find out who we are."
—Tobias Wolff

Whatever you choose to do in life, I hope you make it your own and do it with passion!

When I was climbing the ladder in my direct sales career I was also teaching ten to fifteen hours of aerobic dancing classes a week. I held seven shows a week, was a stepmom to three teenagers, and became a grandmother at age thirty-one. I was passionate about all of it. The plan was to stay healthy and make enough money to buy a home. I wanted to be a positive influence in the lives of my step children. They were going to be the only children I would ever have. Fast-forward to twenty-five years later. The plan, purpose, and persistence has more than paid off. Remember to be patient with yourself. You are a constant work in progress.

6. Positive Support Team PST

> *"Don't allow anyone to tell you what you can and cannot do.*
> *Be tough, be stubborn, love yourself, and find friends*
> *who believe in you. Recognize your victories."*
> —Joan Benoit Samuelson

Surround yourself with people who support your values, ideals, and goals. Let the energy suckers go rain on someone else's parade. Celebrate small successes—they lead to bigger ones. Remember the number one rule of management: behavior that is rewarded will be repeated. Celebrate your success and the successes of people you are encouraging to rise to the top.

Become a "human highlighter" and start bringing out the best in those around you. As a "recovering" aerobics instructor I can tell you that the best exercise you will ever get is bending over to help someone else up!

> *"Follow me . . . I'm right behind you!"*
> —Janet Cronstedt
> Vice President of
> Sales Cookie Lee Jewelry

These six habits feed off each other as they help you rise above the crowd. When you practice your PMA mantra, "feeling good, looking good," you start believing in yourself. That gives you the energy to start expanding your belief systems.

> *"Every blade of grass has its Angel that bends over it*
> *and whispers, 'Grow . . . grow.'"*
> —The Talmud

As you learn and grow you gain an understanding of the value of discipline and how easy it is to break your goals down to do *a little a lot* every day. These disciplines lead to self-confidence and a willingness to take more risks because with risks comes rewards, even if the rewards are gleaning the lesson from that last adventure in learning. The next habit of keeping the passion alive to fuel your plan with purpose requires that you are patient with yourself. Enjoy the journey. Finally, never give up on you. You are a work in progress until you die.

In our local paper this week there was an article about Cliff Garl. Ignoring doubts from his doctor, the ninety-one-year-old soloed in a Cessna 172 and earned his pilot's certificate. There are no figures for students over the age of ninety but there is a good chance he is the only one! Alena Melnyk celebrated her 103rd birthday this past month. Her secret to long life is "keeping busy."

> *"We live on a planet of possibilities, not in a land of limitations!"*
> —Bonnie Dean

Whatever path you choose to rise to the top of your game of life make it your own! In the words of the West Point Cadet Maxim:

Risk more than others think is safe.

> *"Come to the edge." He said. They said "we are afraid."*
> *"Come to the edge." He said. They said "we are afraid."*
> *"Come to the edge." He said. They came.*
> *He pushed them, and they flew!*
> —Guilliaume Apollonaire

Keep five pennies in your pocket. Every time your fingers find them remind yourself that risk is all about making small changes. Simply focus doing *a little a lot*—focus on small change!

> *"It is what we make out of what we have,*
> *not what we are given,*
> *that separates one person from another."*
> —Nelson Mandela

Care more than others think is wise.

People don't care how much you know until they know how much you care about them. At the end of the day we are as rich as the quality of our relationships.

"Kindness in words creates confidence.
Kindness in thinking creates profoundness.
Kindness in giving creates love."

—Lao Tzu

Dream more than others think is practical.
It says in the Bible without dreams and visions we perish. You can't dream big dreams with small thoughts. Create a dream board with pictures of the places you want to see and taste and experience. Place it in a prominent place in your home where you can focus on it daily. Let it be your wishing stone.

Expect more than others think is possible.
Expect laughter, learning, and inspiration every day.
Expect more of your relationships, your career.
Expect more from the people you work with and the people you love.
Most importantly, expect more from yourself!

Life is funny. You generally get what you expect. When you refuse to accept anything less than the best from yourself, your friends, family, and your life's work . . . you often get it!

"The future belongs to those who fuse intelligence with faith,
and who, with courage and determination,
grope their way forward from chance to choice,
from blind adaptation to creative evolution."
— Charles E. Merriam (1876–1953)

"Life should not *be a journey to the grave with the intention of arriving safely in an attractive and well preserved body, but rather to skid in sideways, cigar in hand, favorite beverage in the other, body thoroughly used up, totally worn out, and screaming, 'Whoo-hoo! what a ride!'"*

—Author unknown

"Enjoy the journey!"

—Bonnie Dean

Bonnie Dean

Heard most recently in South Africa on *Cape Town Talk* and *Women Speak,* Bonnie Dean is a frequent quest on KTLA television's *Making IT* morning show doing motivational minutes.

Bonnie is the CCO of Creating CORE Connections, an international events company that focuses on "Staying in Touch with what *Really* Matters" and celebrates the relationships of co-workers, customers, and management.

Bonnie is a Speaker, Coach, Author, Dreamer, Wife, Stepmom, Sister, Aunt, Grandmother, Great-Grandmother, Fairy Godmother to Many.

She is a veg-o-matic blend of Shakespearean actor, improv comic, sitcom starlet, Harvard professor, information architect, Broadway choreographer, Navaho storyteller, circus clown, aerobics instructor, and industrial psychologist. Working only with a suitcase of props, a pair of sparkling tennis shoes, and a "hitch your SUV to a star" attitude, Bonnie Dean is a human hurricane of immense heart and boundless energy who throws off more sparks than a NASA Shuttle launch.

Consider Bonnie for your next convention, training, team event or coaching needs. She turns black-and-white affairs into Technicolor extravaganzas!

Bonnie Dean
Phone: 360.392.8810
www.bonniedean.com

A SPECIAL INTERVIEW

Jim Rohn

David E. Wright (Wright)

It's my sincere pleasure today to welcome Jim Rohn to *Rising to the Top.* Jim has helped motivate and train an entire generation of personal development trainers, as well as hundreds of executives from America's top corporations. He's been described as everything from "master motivator" to a "modern day Will Rodgers," to a legend. Jim has been internationally hailed over the years as one of the most influential thinkers of our time. His professional development seminars have spanned thirty-nine years. He has addressed over six thousand audiences and four million people worldwide. He has authored seventeen different books as well as dozens of audio and video programs. There simply are not enough superlatives when introducing Jim Rohn.

Jim, thank you for taking time to visit with us today.

Jim Rohn (Rohn)

Hey, my pleasure.

Wright

Before we dive into some pretty deep subjects, I know our readers would appreciate an update on your current focus.

Rohn

Well, I'm still involved in world travel—from Asia to South Africa, South America, to Europe, across the United States—which I've been doing for the last forty years and enjoying it very much.

Wright

I've belonged to a political discussion group called Great Decisions, for the last fifteen years. Every year we discuss conditions in Africa and every year we come away with our hands in our pockets, saying we don't know what can be done about it. Is it as bad as we believe?

Rohn

It's a complex continent and who knows what it will finally take. You know, there are some good signs but you're right.

Wright

The problems are just voluminous.

Rohn

I have lectured in all the major cities in South Africa. I've gone there several times over the last twenty years. When I first went they still had Apartheid, now that's all gone. There are some good signs that recovery is under way and I love to see that.

I first lectured in Moscow in Russia, starting about ten years ago and fortunately that was after the walls came tumbling down—they were changing from communism to capitalism. I've made about five lecture tours in Russia in the last ten years, teaching capitalism and personal responsibility and entrepreneurship. It's exciting to go back and see so many of them doing it. They still have a long way to go—there's still push and pull between the old ways and the new ways.

Years and years ago when I went to South America, every country had a dictator. Now they're all gone, for the most part. So there are a lot of improvements that have been made around the world but there is still a long way to go.

Wright

Do you appreciate the United States when you come back in?

Rohn

No doubt about it. This is the place where you can start with so little and still you can start with pennies and make your fortune with some good advice and coaching and a bit of training and personal responsibility and a whole lot of courage. That's extraordinary.

Wright

I spend a lot of time with professionals from all types of industries and I often give career advice when I'm asked.

Would you mind looking back over your career and sharing a story or two that demonstrates some relevant success principles? In other words, to what do you attribute your success in life?

Rohn

I met someone when I was twenty-five; his name was Earl Schoff (this is in most of my recordings and writings). I worked for him for five years. He died at the early age of forty-nine, but during those five years I worked for him, he gave me really a lot of the fundamentals—especially the economic and personal development principles—that revolutionized my life.

When I met him I had only pennies in my pocket, nothing in the bank, and creditors calling once in a while saying, "You told us the check was in the mail." That embarrasses me.

I think what triggered my search to find him was what I call "the Girl Scout story." I was at home alone and heard a knock on my door. I go to the door and there's this Girl Scout selling cookies. She gives me this great presentation (it's the best organization in the world). She goes on and on and she describes the several different flavors available and that the cost is only two dollars. Then she politely asked me to buy.

No problem, I wanted to buy—big problem, I didn't have two dollars. I can remember today that embarrassing moment—I'm a grown man and I'm twenty-five years old; I've had one year of college, I've got a little family started, I live in America, and I don't have two dollars in my pocket.

I didn't want to tell her that, so I lied to her and said, "Hey look, we've already bought lots of Girl Scout cookies, we've still got plenty in the house we haven't eaten yet.

She said, "Oh, that's wonderful! Thank you very much," and she leaves.

When she leaves, I say to myself, "I don't want to live like this anymore. I mean how low you can get, lying to a Girl Scout? That's got to be the bottom, right?

I called it "the day that turns your life around." Everybody can look back at some of those days when you made a unique decision at a particular time and you were never the same again. That was one of those days.

Shortly after that I met this incredible mentor I went to work for—Earl Schoff. Using the things he taught me, I became a millionaire by the age of thirty-two.

It doesn't take much if you get the right information and put it to work and are willing to accept refinement, keep up your studies, and engage primarily in what we call "personal development"—becoming more valuable. For economics, personal development makes you more valuable to the marketplace. Personal development also makes you become more valuable as a father, a mother, a parent, a friend, a business colleague, and as a citizen.

Personal development is the subject I have talked most about seeing how valuable you can be to yourself, to your community, and to those around you.

I've got a little economic phase I use that says, "We get paid for bringing value to the marketplace." And the first part of that is the value you bring such as a product, but the biggest part of what you bring is how valuable you become through personal development. I say, "To climb the ladder of success, work harder on yourself than you do on your job." If you work hard on your job, you can make a living, if you work hard on yourself, you can make a fortune.

I learned those very fundamental ideas when I was twenty-five. Fortunately I discovered them at twenty-five rather than at fifty-five. Fifty-five is okay and seventy-five is still okay but gosh, it's good to learn them at the age of twenty-five when you can really put them to work. These ideas revolutionized my life and they formed the foundation of what I've shared now all these years in so many forms.

Wright

I've only heard the name Schoff twice. You just mentioned it and when I was in junior high school in seventh and eighth and ninth grades, one of my mentors was a coach named Schoff. He was a real mentor. This guy was just a fine, fine, man.

Rohn

The same man, Earl Schoff, influenced Mary Kay (the lady who started Mary Kay Cosmetics) and me back in 1955–1956. Those were the early, early years. Mary Kay went on to become a superstar. What he shared with me just transformed my life.

Wright

You're known throughout the world as a personal development expert. In practical terms what does that really mean?

Rohn

Well, there's a phase that says, "Success is not something you pursue, success is something you attract"—by becoming an attractive person. Currently I'm sharing it like this: to really do well you need multiple skills. If you've just got one skill, it's too risky economically. For example, a guy has worked for a company for twenty years and the division he works for goes out of business. He's lost his job and he tells us he's in financial trouble. The reason is that, even after twenty years of working, he only had one skill. If he had taken an accounting course or some other course two nights a week he would have had another skill to market. There's so much available out there that can increase your value to the marketplace.

I started learning these extra skills: finding good people, sales, finding a product I could believe in, and talk about its merits until somebody said Yes, follow up, and get referrals. Then I learned to build an organization. I then learned organization—getting people to work together. I needed to learn to get a team and work together. Then I learned recognition—I learned to reward people for small steps of progress.

The biggest skill I learned was communication. I got involved in training, showing people how the job works, and then I got involved in teaching. I taught setting goals, personal development leadership, and communication skills. My theme for that was, "You need both job skills and life skills," because just learning how to set goals revolutionized my life.

Then the ultimate in communication is learning to inspire— helping people see themselves as better than they are, transport them in to the future, paint the possibilities, and then use your own testimony. Say, "Hey if I can do it, you can do it."

So you're starting with pennies, you're behind, the creditors are calling; but that's not really what's important. What's important is the decision today to start the journey of self-improvement. I think that theme has been paramount in all of my teaching and training during the last forty years—work harder on yourself than you do on your job.

In leadership, I teach that to attract attractive people, you must be attractive. So it's a constant pursuit of self-development and personal development.

The theme during my career, teaching and training during the past forty years is: communication, managing your time, managing your money, and learning to inspire.

Wright

You know, I have my own opinion about how difficult it is for people to change whether it involves a health issue or dieting, for example. Do you believe that people can really change and why is change so difficult?

Rohn

Give easy steps. For example, if you want to change your health and you say, "I've got to do something that will make me healthy. My momma taught that an apple a day was healthy," why not start there?

If you don't start with something simple, you can forget the rest of the complicated stuff. Sometimes it's good to do it with someone else. I've found in all my entrepreneurial business projects during the last forty years, it's more inspiring to say, "Let's go do it," than to say, "I'm going to go do it." Get together with someone and say, "Let's get healthy, let's exercise, let's go to the gym, let's climb a mountain." The "let's" is what's very powerful. A lot of things are pretty tough to do all by yourself.

Wright

In the past there've been some major scandals in corporate America. I know you've counseled many high profiled executives over the years. Is there a leadership crisis in America? What do you think has contributed to this kind of moral failure?

Rohn

No, it's always been such from the beginning of recorded history, when there were just four people on earth. You know there was the great scandal of brother who killed brother (Cain and Abel). So it's not a current phenomenon—it's not a twenty-first century phenomenon. Even the Old Testament records good kings and bad kings—those who "did right in the sight of the Lord" and those who led the people into idolatry. You know, it's just not unusual.

My best explanation is the great adventure started back according to the Storyteller. God created all these angels and then gave them the dignity of choice, and a third of them decided to go with Lucifer and make a run on God's throne. They didn't win but it started what I call "the adventure of the Creator and the spoiler." And then I further describe it with the concept that the adventure of our life seems to be that opposites are in conflict and we are in the middle. But this is what makes a great adventure.

Illness tries to overcome your health, but if you work on your health you can overcome your illness. If, however, you let up the least little bit, sure enough, illness creeps up and takes away some more of your health.

Regarding liberty and tyranny in the world, for a while there was more tyranny than liberty. Since the walls came down in Berlin I am hopeful that there will be more liberty than tyranny in the future.

But whether its politics or whether it's corporations, it doesn't matter, the temptation is always there—the drama is always there. Should we do the right thing or would it be okay to cross the line? I use the following illustration sometimes: When I was a little kid I saw a cartoon of a little boy. The little boy had an angel—a little angel—on one shoulder, and a little devil on the other shoulder. Both of them were whispering in his ear. The little devil said, "Go ahead and do it, it will be okay."

The little angels says, "No, no, it *won't* be okay."

The little devil says, "Yes, yes, go ahead, it's okay; nobody will know."

The little angel says, "No, no, no!"

That little cartoon appeared back when I was a kid. It describes the concept of opposites in conflict and that's what makes an adventure.

There wouldn't be positive without negative it doesn't seem like. And you couldn't win if you couldn't lose. If you took a football today and walked out to the stadium and we followed you and in the football stadium you took the football and walked across the goal line, would we all cheer and call it a touchdown? The answer is No, that's silly. It's not a touchdown until you face the three-hundred-pounders. If you can muscle past them (they want to smash your face in the dirt) and if you can dance by the secondary, on a special day, we call it a touchdown, and maybe you win the championship.

That's the deal—opposites are in conflict. We're tempted every day, whether it's the little things or something big and major. You come to the intersection and the light is yellow and it starts to turn red. Some little voice may whisper to you, "Go ahead, you're late—you can make it." But if you try running that light you may wind up dead. If you say, "No, I'll be more cautious, then you live a little bit longer."

So it's not that we're not involved in this push and pull. It happens at the high echelons of corporate America. Little voices whisper in a collective way around the boardroom, and the board members decide to cross the line. They think, "It looks like we can get by with it—we can put it off shore or we can play some games here and we'll be okay" or "If we want this stock to grow and necessity demands it, we probably skate the line a little bit." That happens in the poorest of homes and it happens in the riches of homes. It happens in the boardroom and it happens on Main Street and it happens in the back alley. So it doesn't really matter where it is, temptation is always there. But that's what makes the adventure—to see if you can handle the temptation and do more right than wrong—have a longer list of virtues than mistakes—then you win.

Wright

I recently read an article you wrote about attitude. In it you said attitude determines how much of the future we're allowed to see. This is a fascinating thing to say. Will you elaborate on this thought?

Rohn

Well, it's attitude about four things:

1. *How you feel about the past.* Some people carry the past around like a burden. They continually live and dwell on their past mistakes. They live in the past (i.e., their past failures) and it just drains away all the energy they could apply to something much more positive. We have to have a good healthy attitude about the past. The key on that is

just to learn from it. Hey, here's where I messed up, I've got that corrected now, and I'm going to make the changes for the future. We call that "drawing on the past" as a good school of experience to make corrections in errors in judgment or whatever put you in a bad place.

2. *How you feel about the future.* We need to look back for experience but we need to look ahead for inspiration. We need to be inspired by the goals we set for ourselves and for our family, the goals we've set for friendship, lifestyle, becoming wealthy, powerful, and influential, and as a unique citizen, those goals that get us up early and keep us up late, fire up the fuel of our imagination, and how can we accomplish them.

3. *How you feel about everybody.* You can't succeed by yourself. It takes everybody for each of us to be successful. Each of us needs all of us. One person doesn't make an economy; one person doesn't make a symphony orchestra. So you have to have that unique sense of the value of everybody and that it really does take everybody for any one person to be successful.

4. *How you feel about yourself.* This is the most important one. At the end of the day evaluate yourself: "I pushed it to the limit, I did everything I could, I made every call, I stretched as far as I could." If that's true, then you can lie down and sleep a good sleep. Solomon wrote, "The sleep of the laboring man is sweet . . ." (Ecclesiastes 5:12). This describes people who put in the work—who work hard either with their hands or with their mind or with their ability to communicate, whatever it is—so at the end of the day they feel good about themselves. Nothing is more powerful than high self-esteem. It builds self-confidence, which builds success.

Those five attitudes really do give you a promising look at the future. But if you're always being pulled back by the past or distracted because you find it difficult to manage your life with people you have to associate with, that's tough. And the better you can handle that and realize the law of averages says you're going to be around some good people and some bad people, and you're going to be around some ambitious people and some not so ambitious, the better off you'll be. You've got to learn to take it all in stride.

Then knowing that you're on track for better health and you're on track for becoming financially independent. You haven't quite got it solved, but you're on track for the management of your time and your money. And your attitude toward that really creates high inspiration that the future's going to multiply several times better than the past.

Wright

I don't normally like to frame a question in the negative but I thought it would be interesting to get your prospective on mistakes that people make in life and in business. If you had to name the top three on a list of mistakes people make that kept them from succeeding or living a fulfilled life, what would they be?

Rohn

Well, number one mistake economically is not to understand that people can make you wealthy. And all you have to do is just figure out how to do that. For example: Johnny mows Mrs. Brown's lawn and she pays five dollars. One day it occurs to him, "If I get my friend Paul to mow this lawn, Mrs. Brown would pay five dollars. I would give Paul four dollars and keep one for myself because I got the job." Instantly Johnny has now moved to a higher level of economics that says this is how you become wealthy.

A little phrase that philosophically and economically changed my life is: "Profits are better than wages." Wages make you a living but profits make you a fortune. You don't have to be General Motors, you don't have to be high in the industrial complex society to understand this concept; that's why it's so powerful to teach capitalism, how to buy and sell and how to sell and buy.

I've got so many stories of people I've helped in my seminars who started with pennies and now they're rich. That's the key—learning how to employ other people. First do it yourself—learn how to do it yourself—then find a need someone has and get someone else to render the service, and then someone else and then someone else. Teach them the same, and the principles of economics and capitalism. The knowledge of how to go from having pennies to gaining a fortune is so simple.

When I taught it to the Russians they couldn't believe how simple it was. I said, "Capital is any value you set aside to be invested in an enterprise that brings value to the marketplace hoping to make a profit"—that's capitalism. They couldn't believe I could put it in one sentence.

Wright

I can't either.

Rohn

I teach kids how to have two bicycles—one to ride and one to rent. It doesn't take long to make a profit. If you're halfway bright, if you get just a little advice to give you a chance to start, you'll make it.

I see capitalism in two parts—one is capital time, the other is capital money. If you wisely learn to invest capital money you can make a fortune. And then together with that, if you can learn to invest capital time you can also amass a fortune. You set aside time to be invested in an enterprise.

I started that part-time when I was twenty-five years old, all those years ago in 1955. I took about fifteen to twenty hours a week part-time and invested it in a capital enterprise. By the time I was thirty-two I was a millionaire. It didn't take much money because I only invested $200, which I borrowed. That was my capital money, but the other was my capital time. Once I learned how to invest both and then learned how to teach and train and inspire other people to do the same, it totally changed my life.

I don't have to worry about social security—I developed my own social security. It's interesting that they're not teaching that today when social security is such a main topic. We've got to let our young people put aside some of that withholding and put it in a personal account. How about teaching them how to be financially independent? Who's doing that? John Kennedy said," Don't ask what your country can do for you . . ." Don't ask what the social security program can do for you . . . Why not ask what you can do for your country—or social security? Could I mow Mrs. Brown's lawn and collect five dollars and do it part-time? Then could I get someone else to do it and then someone else to do another job, and finally work my way from the pennies in my pocket to the fortune that I could have because this is America—the land of opportunity?

It's startling how simple it is in concept and how really easy it is in practice; but the results can be phenomenal. I got such great early results that I never did look back, from age twenty-five until today.

For me it's fun to teach it. I've been teaching it now for all these years and I've got some testimonials where I helped people start, just like I started with pennies and now they're rich. It's just exciting.

One of the great exciting experiences is to have your name appear in somebody's testimonial: "Here's the person who found me, here's the person who taught me, here's the person who wouldn't let me quit, gave me more reasons for staying than for leaving. Here's the person who believed in me until I could believe in myself," then they mention your name. I call that big time, and you can't buy it with money. You have to simply earn it by sharing ideas with somebody that makes a difference in their life. And I love to do it.

Wright

This is the definition of great mentors.

Rohn

Yes, I love to be that. Hopefully my books and tapes and my personal appearances have done that during the last forty years.

Wright

I'd like to go back to the issue of personal development and change. Considering the issues most Americans face in this modern era with all of our technology, where would you advise most people to focus their energy if they could only change one thing about themselves?

Rohn

I'd advise them to start figuring out to how to learn another skill, and then another skill. Then it would be good to learn another language. People who know more than one language receive good pay. Some of my business colleagues who speak three or four languages make three or four million a year. Not that this is a guarantee, but that's just an idea for self-improvement. Learn something beyond what you know now because it could be something that you can cash in on, maybe sooner than you think.

Wright

Not to mention the fact that you're talking for the first time to another whole culture and look what you could learn. I've always been fascinated by the Chinese culture.

Rohn

I would also suggest that people develop wise use of their time and then wise use of their money. I teach kids to not spend more than seventy cents out of every dollar—ten cents for charity or church, ten cents for active capital (i.e., the two bicycles, one to ride and one to rent concept), then passive capital of 10 percent. Let someone else use it (you provide the capital that will pay you dividends, increase in stock or whatever). I call it "seventy-ten-ten and ten." Then I teach not to buy the second car until you've bought the second house. Cars won't make you rich but houses will make you rich. I love to teach that.

A lady called me from Mexico not long ago and said, "Mr. Rohn, I'm now shopping for my third car because I just finished paying for my third house." She started listening to my training ten years ago. She not only uses it, she teaches it. Down in Mexico she makes about $40,000 a month, which down there is just staggering.

But it's fun—it's been fun for me over the years to have stories like that. I use my own story as an inspiration not only for myself but also for the people who listen to my lectures. And then it's fun to watch people actually grab hold of something and turn it into success.

Wright

Jim, it's been a sincere joy having this enlightening conversation with you today. I really appreciate and thank you so much again for taking the time to be with us on *Rising to the Top*.

Rohn

I appreciate it and I thank you for calling.

Wright

Thank you so much.

Jim Rohn

JIM ROHN is a philosopher, motivational counselor, business executive, and best-selling author. He has been recognized as the greatest motivational speaker of all time. He is one of the world's most sought-after success counselors and business philosophers. Some of his most thought-provoking topics include: sales and entrepreneurial skills, leadership, sales and marketing, success, and personal development.

Jim Rohn has conducted seminars for over thirty-nine years and addressed over six thousand audiences and four million people worldwide. He is a recipient of the 1985 National Speakers Association CPAE Award. He's authored over seventeen different books, audio, and video programs. Rohn has been internationally hailed over the years as one of the most influential thinkers of our time.

Revealing contemporary success secrets in a way that is both accessible and practical, Jim ignites enthusiasm and a can-do attitude in all who hear him speak. He approaches the subjects of personal and professional success by asking four questions: Why? Why not? Why not you? Why not now? He answers these questions and reveals practical, perceptive secrets for success and productivity. His special style, laced with witticisms and anecdotes, captivates listeners. Among his most thought-provoking topics are: sales and entrepreneurial skills, leadership, sales and marketing, success, and personal development.

Jim Rohn
www.jimrohn.com

GIVE YOURSELF A PROMOTION
How Personal Marketing Can Take You Straight to the Top

Don Hobbs and Greg Herder

The gold blazers and brown slacks that symbolized early '80s real estate were more than a fashion faux pas—to us, anyway. In a way, they were an indirect impetus to start our company. We formed Hobbs/Herder Advertising in 1986 when we recognized the need for real estate agents to differentiate themselves from one another due to the growing popularity of franchises that rendered individual agents as one and the same. After all, if you were one of those agents wearing the gold blazer and brown pants, what good does the company's branding do for you if no one is asking for you personally?

In 2006, Hobbs/Herder Advertising celebrated its twentieth year as experts in personal marketing. Throughout that time we've earned a reputation as pioneers in personal marketing with a specialty in real estate, but our knowledge and philosophies regarding personal marketing extend to any industry in which a personal "brand" can set you apart from the competition.

Put simply, personal marketing is building the brand called *you*. Anyone can benefit from it—real estate agents, lawyers, doctors, accountants, insurance agents, and any professional service provider, which includes anyone in management. Personal marketing allows professionals to differentiate themselves within their fields so they stand out in their highly competitive marketplace. The end result is that by doing so, they attract the best clients and opportunities seem to flow to them.

Attracting Business Instead of Chasing It

Before we get into personal marketing, let's take a look at branding as a whole. Think about companies like Nike, Coca-Cola or Rolex. Their ads aren't geared around the qualities of their products; they're about positioning themselves as attractive brands in the minds of consumers. They try to entertain you—make you laugh, make you cry, make you feel good. In the process, they capture a spot in your heart that makes you feel better about buying their product over a competitor's almost identical product.

Personal marketing does the same thing for individuals. It's about building relationships with prospective clients before you ever meet them in person and often, before they even know they have a need for your product or service.

Think about it for a second. Let's say you need an accountant. You don't know an accountant personally—all you see in the phone book is a list of names. Now, all things being equal, wouldn't you rather work with someone you know? Wouldn't you rather work with someone you have a positive feeling about? That's personal branding. It sets businesses apart from their competition and creates a preference toward doing business with them. There's another part to this "someone you know." If we see an individual's name often, that person must be good. How do we know? Because we have heard the name many times! This also implies another interesting marketing idea—if you've never previously heard of a particular business or person (i.e., the accountant in our example here), how good could that person or business possibly be?

Sales vs. Marketing

This is the key difference between sales and marketing. You can be an incredible salesperson, but it doesn't really matter if you don't have anyone to talk to. Marketing is the process by which you attract business rather than chasing it. You do so by making yourself attractive to your prospective clients and most importantly, creating a perceived difference between yourself and your competition. Remember that "perceived" is the key word there. The difference between facial tissues is probably unnoticeable to most people. Then again, most people don't ask for a tissue. They ask for a Kleenex. That's the power of branding.

This is not to say that sales skills are not important. But any salesperson or businessperson will tell you that chasing deals can be draining. Do it long enough and it will lead to burnout. Where marketing fits in is by delivering clients to you—making your phone ring with prospects who are already predisposed to working with you. Here's one simple way to boil it down: When was the last time Nike called you trying to sell you a pair of shoes? Never, of course. They don't need to because their marketing has people lining up outside sporting goods stores to buy the new models on the day they are released. Now, are Nike shoes really that much better than the competition? Are they *any* better than the competition? Who knows? All we know is that we've got to have them.

Emotion vs. Fact

So we've established that a key to marketing is differentiation. In personal marketing applications, unless your product or service is completely unique, the only thing that makes you different is you. So the question then becomes how you differentiate yourself from the competition. This is where most people get themselves in trouble. When you ask a salesperson or a small business owner to tell you how he or she is different, you immediately hear a sales pitch. You'll hear about the years of experience these people have. They'll tell you about the level of service they provide. And they'll tell you about how well they know and understand their product.

This is akin to Nike using a thirty-second television commercial to tell you about the quality that goes into their shoe manufacturing process. Nobody cares.

The lesson here is that when people give you an opportunity to prove how you are different, you have to wow them. Think back to what we wrote about earlier—the commercials that make you laugh or make you cry. What are they tapping into to do that?

In a word: emotion.

Emotion is everything when it comes to marketing. As much as we would like to tell ourselves otherwise, we do not make buying decisions based on logic and rationale and facts. We make them on emotion. For proof, let's go back to the Nike example. You've probably bought at least one pair of Nikes at some point in your life. Now, before you did so, did you investigate to see what kinds of materials were used to make them? Did you look them up in the *Consumer Reports* magazine to determine how long the soles would last versus competing brands? No, of course not. You saw a commercial, thought they were cool and told yourself you had to have them. End of story.

This is the power of emotion-based marketing. You have to tell a story. You have to set yourself apart in a memorable way. It might seem obvious, but to become great at personal marketing, you have to be willing to get personal. You have to reveal the parts of yourself, your life, and your philosophies that make you interesting. You need to become a storyteller, engaging the reader in your world. Only then do you have the power to captivate an audience and attract business toward you.

Narrow Your Focus to Broaden Your Appeal

When we—Don Hobbs and Greg Herder—joined forces to create Hobbs/Herder Advertising, we had several choices. Having both previously worked with Jim Rohn, we were heavily influenced by his philosophies. From those experiences we knew that whatever we did, we wanted to touch people and help change their lives for the better. We had a specific—but basic at that time—knowledge of personal marketing and we could have opened our doors to anyone. We chose real estate professionals instead. Why? Who knows? The world was wide open—we could have selected lawyers or doctors or plumbers or tax accountants or any number of specialties. We chose real estate, and that decision has worked out very well for us, although we're confident we could have been just as successful if we'd picked any of the aforementioned fields.

Another thing we're confident about is that if we hadn't chosen any one particular focus, we'd probably be out of business right now. Why? Because you don't become successful trying to be all things to all people. Having a specialty builds perceived value for your product or service. This is called "niche marketing." It immediately positions you as an expert. Whether you take your car to Amoco to fix its transmission or if you have a cardiac specialist investigate your heart murmur, you expect more and therefore pay more to specialists. You're buying the security of their expertise. Take Lasik eye surgery, for example. If you're going to have someone slice your eyes open, do you want just any eye doctor doing that? No way! You want a Lasik specialist, and chances are you're willing to pay a premium for that added peace of mind.

"But wait!" people say. "If I position myself as a specialist, I'm eliminating a huge portion of the overall market. Wouldn't I have to be crazy to do that?"

We hear this all the time. The reality is you'd have to be crazy *not* to do it. If you don't niche market yourself as an expert in any one field, what compelling reason do you have for anyone to choose you over the competition? When you try to be all things to all people, you end up being remembered for nothing. Meanwhile, the specialist's business thrives because people know they need the services provided and they perceive that they cannot obtain the same level of service, knowledge, and insight elsewhere. They don't forget the specialist.

In our industry, one shining example immediately comes to mind. His name is Allan Domb and we helped him establish himself as the "Condo King" of Philadelphia. Now, could Allan sell houses? Of course he could. Is there that much difference between houses and condos? Of course there isn't. But, by positioning himself as a condo *expert*, he stands out from the crowd. And if you're in the market to buy or sell a condo in Philadelphia, there's only one name you need to know. You can either work with an agent who tries to be everything to everyone, or you can work with the condo expert—Allan Domb. No wonder Allan has sold hundreds of condos every year for the last fifteen or more years.

Make Yourself Stand Out

Choosing a niche isn't easy. It's a difficult decision that requires analysis of your business, your market, and your objectives. And it starts by looking at your choices. There are as many ways to segment the population as there are people. From the very specific, to the very general, the possibilities for niche marketing are only limited by your imagination.

To get some ideas, take a look at yourself, your family, and your past and current clients. Think about how you would categorize these people in terms of geography, lifestyle, hobbies, occupation, ethnicity, etc. Pay attention to any trends or patterns. Major overlapping in any area could be a possible market niche. The more you, your clients, and the people you know have in common in a specific area, the more likely it is that you could turn this feature into a unique marketing concept. This leads you to an important question: which niche is right for you?

When looking for a niche to market in, make sure it allows you to offer a unique benefit. To determine if this niche will work with you, consider these three things:

Personality Fit. Do you feel totally comfortable with the people in this group? Do you understand them? Do they feel totally comfortable with you? Ideally, you should find a niche that fits your style. Think about the things that you and our current clients have in common to help narrow the field.

Competition. Are any other people targeting this group? Make sure that the niche you choose is one that is the best fit for you. Beware of looking like you're jumping on the bandwagon. Even if the group is large enough to support competitors, make sure no one person has 30 percent or more of the market share. Taking on a dominant competitor head-on is the surest way to fail.

Size. How many sales or potential sales does this group of people represent per year? How much is your time worth? You must be sure you can get enough business from the group to support the energy and funds you'll need to devote to marketing to make it pay off.

The Personal Marketer's Toolkit

How you deliver your unique marketing message to your target market depends on a variety of factors, including the size of your target market. But for most individual businesspeople the best place to start is in direct mail. You can build very powerful relationships with prospective clients through consistent, targeted direct mail campaigns. It's something we've been doing since day one at Hobbs/Herder.

The product that we introduced and have pioneered for the last twenty years is the high-quality, full-color personal brochure. Now, of course there were brochures before we came along, but they never really included the key points we've covered above: emotion, vision, and differentiation, printed in a format that demonstrates quality and attention to detail. Not surprisingly, most brochures created by sales or businesspeople end up reading like a sales presentation committed to paper. Where we revolutionized the concept is by infusing the personal brochure with emotion and personality, so that it created a brand identity in readers' minds and started the process of making them want to do business with our clients over any of their competitors.

Let's establish one key point right from the start—an effective personal brochure is not a sales tool. It's better viewed as a relationship builder that breaks down barriers and allows prospective clients to get a feel for who you are. We sometimes refer to it as a "cup of coffee," as if it is designed to reveal the personal anecdotes and history that you would discuss if meeting someone for the first time over a cup of coffee. The objective is for someone to read your personal brochure, feel like they have met you, and have a clear understanding of what you do. The feeling that they know you becomes a key point of differentiation when they need your services at a later time.

Your personal brochure tells the story that is the backbone or centerpiece of your entire marketing campaign. Because it is such a powerful branding tool, it should replace your common business card. Every time you meet someone, you should hand out your personal brochure and invite the person to read about you. Wait until you see the reaction you'll get as your brochure makes an extremely positive first impression. You should also mail your personal brochure to your target market every six months, even if you know people have read it before. That's because consistency and repetition are an essential element of successful personal marketing. You cannot sit back and hope that people remember you from just a few mailings a year.

At Hobbs/Herder we have experienced great success utilizing oversized postcards that we call "PowerKards" to keep our clients' image in front of their target market on a regular basis. There are several advantages to this type of marketing. For one, it is relatively inexpensive to create and to mail. Two, a PowerKard cannot "not work." We know that's an odd way to phrase it, but due to its immediate delivery of your image—no envelopes to open or decisions to make on the part of the recipient—we believe it's the most accurate way to say it. Due to its oversized nature, a PowerKard stands out in the day's mail and will get read. And that's all you're hoping for. If you can deliver your name and image to your target market with frequency and consistency, your brand will build in the minds of your targets. You should send a PowerKard to your target market two to three times every month.

Consistency is Key

Left to their own devices, most people will probably assume that they need to develop a new PowerKard for every mailing and then determine that it all sounds like too much time, effort, and money to be worthwhile. They'd be wrong on all fronts.

Here's another beautiful thing about the PowerKard—you create it once and it allows you the flexibility to deliver various messages to your target market while also possessing the necessary consistency to build your brand. This is achieved by leaving a portion of the card blank in order to be overprinted with your individual message. This allows you to print high-quality, full-color "masters" in bulk to save on printing costs and then selectively mail each message individually by having it overprinted on the cards in black ink. This scenario keeps the focus on you and your brand while also allowing you to deliver individual marketing messages and demonstrate your market knowledge to those people in your direct mail "farm."

Our real estate clients use this approach to inform homeowners of newly listed homes and recently sold properties, to provide market updates, to offer special reports, and much more. The flexibility of the PowerKard allows freedom to use it any way you choose without sacrificing quality in the process. A similar approach could be used by any independent businessperson.

Exploring Mass Media

In addition to direct mail, a personal marketing campaign can include print advertising (newspapers and magazines), outdoor advertising (billboards, bus benches, etc.) as well as radio and now television, thanks to inexpensive cable television advertising. Cable television is much more affordable than you probably think it is, and it can make a big impression on people. When a prospective client sees you on television, there is a sense of legitimacy and credibility that cannot be conveyed via other media options. What you want to create is the most well-rounded campaign possible that delivers your name and image consistently. You want prospective clients saying, "I see this guy everywhere!"

Reaping the Rewards

The objective for any personal marketing campaign is to establish your name and brand within your target market and to generate a steady flow of leads while avoiding the draining process of continually chasing prospective clients. This allows you to remain focused on your real expertise. Personal marketing leverages you by allowing you to *attract* business and *conduct* business simultaneously. An effective, well-rounded campaign works for you round the clock, so you don't have to.

No matter what your ultimate objective, personal marketing allows you the time and energy to live a better life; whether that means having more free time and balance in your life or improving your efficiency to increase your income potential, investing in yourself through personal marketing is the answer.

Attitude is Everything

One key to effective personal marketing, however, is having faith in your plan and allowing it the time and resources to succeed. We have always believed that a person's attitude plays a significant role in the success or failure of a campaign. Here's the key—adopting a marketing mindset isn't something that can happen overnight. It requires change. But as our mentor Jim Rohn taught us, things won't change for you until you change the way you think.

Adopting a personal marketing mindset is one change that can radically alter the course of your life. We've embraced and lived these philosophies from the first time we heard them so many years ago, and we've witnessed firsthand hundreds of accounts of how personal marketing can change people's lives for the better.

At Hobbs/Herder we practice what we preach. We market our company in regional and national publications. We even have a personal brochure that tells about how the company was formed during a fishing trip to a remote Montana stream; but that was only the beginning. By adopting an abundance mentality, we've been able to not only grow our business for more than twenty years, but we've also had the opportunity and good fortune to be in a line of work where we impact so many people's lives.

If there's one thing we've learned through it all, it's that you can have more in life because you can become more. Jim Rohn taught us this lesson many years ago and we prove it each and every day. The truth of the matter is that we are in a position to create anything we want in life. Here in the United States, anything truly is possible. We're very fortunate to be where we are. Once you begin to operate from an abundance mentality—a belief that opportunity is everywhere, there is enough for all and you can get more than your share—you really start to see more opportunities.

It's Not About the Time You Have

One of the major limitations we allow to confine us is time. People are always talking about how they don't have enough time in the day to achieve real success. But to those who feel that way, I ask: Does Bill Gates get more hours each day? Do your competitors have even one more hour in the day? Of course not. We all—rich and poor, happy and unhappy, regular Joes and CEOs of Fortune 500 companies—

have exactly the same amount of time, which means that what it really boils down to is how you look at it.

At Hobbs/Herder Advertising, we believe success isn't about having more time or working harder. It's about getting more from the time you have. The way to do that is to change the way you think about your time and set up systems that allow you to maximize it. Personal marketing is the answer.

Don Hobbs and Greg Herder

DON HOBBS AND GREG HERDER are co-founders of Hobbs/Herder Advertising, a company widely recognized in the industry as a leader and pioneer in personal marketing and business systems for real estate professionals. Since 1986, Hobbs/Herder has trained thousands of agents, managers, and brokers to reach new heights of success.

Don and Greg are renowned for their influence on the industry and they speak to thousands of agents every year about personal marketing systems and strategies to take their business to the next level. They also regularly contribute their expertise to several industry publications. Known for their dynamic style and presentation of immediately usable information, Don and Greg are dedicated to helping real estate professionals increase their profits and reap greater personal satisfaction from their careers.

Today, Don and Greg are just as passionate as ever about making a positive impact on the real estate industry and on individual agents. From private, in-office events to intensive three-day seminars, the team of real estate marketing experts Don and Greg have gathered at Hobbs/Herder Training remain devoted to improving the lives and careers of real estate professionals around the world.

Don Hobbs and Greg Herder
Hobbs/Herder Advertising
2240 University Dr.
Newport Beach, CA 92660
Phone: 800.999.6090
Phone: 949.515.5000
E-mail: Info@HobbsHerder.com
www.HobbsHerder.com

THE P.O.W.E.R. OF LEADERSHIP

Doug Luffborough

THE INTERVIEW

David Wright (Wright)

Today we're talking with Doug Luffborough. Doug is CEO of Luffborough & Associates. He is also founder and Chief Managing Consultant of a community-based nonprofit organization, Turning the Hearts Center, in which he empowers youth and encourages family development.

Doug, we're so glad you're taking the time today to talk with us on *Rising to the Top*.

Doug Luffborough (Luffborough)

Thank you for having me. "Rising to the top" in every area of my life has helped me reach goals that I used to dream about.

Wright

So tell me about your family background.

Luffborough

I'm the oldest of four and was raised by a single parent—my mother—who was a housekeeper. I grew up with humble beginnings and really struggled as a child growing up and trying to understand my place in the world. Unfortunately, I had no male role models in my life and at a young age I grew up quickly in order to raise my two brothers and my sister. Life for me during those days meant sharing the same bed with my brother, during the wintertime sleeping with our coats on because we did not have heat or electricity in the house, and eating bread and butter during meal times.

We grew up in Worcester, Massachusetts. Even though we were poor, my mother was a strong advocate for education, which was of paramount importance in turning my life around. For me, graduating from high school and attending college was my key to "rising to the top." My mother would always say that "education is the key" to our success in life.

Growing up in a single parent household, life was very difficult for me. As a youngster I didn't have many positive role models who completed college or were community leaders. In many cases, many of my role models were negative and did not even finish high school.

Because my family was so poor and I didn't have nice clothes to wear to school, I felt inferior to the other students and that I did not belong in school. Because of my low socio-economic status and constant feelings of insecurity, in elementary school I developed a speech impediment—I stuttered. As a young child I withdrew from anyone who wanted to help me and I was made fun of in school.

Wright

Did you like school?

Luffborough

No, at first I didn't like school. I was one of the students who, if possible, would come late to class and when I did arrive I would always prefer to sit at the back of the classroom. I was a young man with a big chip on my shoulder because I did not fit in with the other students. When you don't fit in with your peers, or feel that you don't belong, one of two things usually happen—you withdraw or you rebel. For me, I started to rebel, mainly because I was told I had a learning disability and had problems in both reading and speaking. I had to leave the classroom in the afternoons to receive one-on-one help in reading, writing, and math.

Many kids made fun of me when I was younger. Sometimes I felt like my second name was "Stupid." There's that old saying that, "Sticks and stones may break my bones but names will never hurt me," but now that I'm grown and I have had the opportunity to work with so many other young people across the nation, I realize that what people say—especially what youngsters say to each other—can be very damaging. Unless it's corrected at a very young age it stays with you long into adulthood. Sometimes it's very hard to turn that around or to identify that it was the source of the inferior mindset or complex.

For me, staying back in the third grade and having to go out of the classroom for extra help for reading and writing damaged my self-esteem and self-image. I felt insignificant, as if my life did not matter. I had a very hard time looking people in the face when I was going through elementary school. It wasn't until high school and college when I identified that those behaviors came from this time in my life.

Wright

When I was a sophomore in high school we were all laughing about this girl and boy who professed their love for each other and we all said it was "puppy love." But a minister told us, "Yes, but it's love to the puppy." So during those years when you're young you learn a lot of lessons.

What helped you build confidence in yourself?

Luffborough

When I was eight, my mother made me take violin lessons. That was not typical because here we were, a really poor African-American family in a predominately Caucasian community, who did not have lights or heat and struggled to find our next meal, yet my brother and I took private violin lessons for ten years.

Through playing the violin I was able to learn, value, and appreciate hard work, discipline, focus, and passion. I was able to build up my self-esteem; I was really able to do very well playing the violin because it was a kinesthetic activity. I started to see changes in my life such as my behavior in school and willingness to get to know other people. Playing the violin gave me meaning because I found something that gave my life purpose and helped me realize that I could do something with my life.

There are three types of learners in the world—auditory, visual, and kinesthetic. At a very young age I came to realize that I learned more by doing. Many kinesthetic learners get mistakenly labeled as having Attention Deficit Hyperactivity Disorder (ADHD) and other problems when learning and teaching styles are different. The U.S. school system is traditionally set up to educate our kids in a very auditory and visual way as opposed to appealing to a kinesthetic learner.

One of the other things that helped me turn around was that my mother is a woman of faith. Faith was eventually transferred to my life and helped me put my trust in God.

Those were the two biggest factors in changing my life around. Playing the violin helped me step outside of my community and outside of what was happening at home. My faith and belief in God gave me reason to celebrate and to believe that all things are possible to those who believe. As the sun sets, the sun also rises and with it comes unlimited opportunities for individuals and families to rise to the top! But you can't quit! My motto to success is simple—"Quitting is not an option . . . if what you are doing is not working, change your approach."

Wright

At the age of ten what were your life goals?

Luffborough

My mom is my biggest inspiration in my life and I think it's very important for young people, as they're growing up, to find someone who can mentor them. Find a mentor who is modeling the advice they are giving you. That person has to emulate what their goals and aspirations are. For me it was my mom. She was a tremendous influence, even though she was a housekeeper. She was a housekeeper because it was the best way to spend time with her children and help raise them. Another part of rising to the top is knowing how to act and carry yourself around others. My mom would often refer to that as having "good home-training." Doors open when you model proper business and personal etiquette.

One of the things my mom would do when she would go to clean her employers' very elegant, big homes, was to take my siblings and me with her. This was how she taught us a solid work ethic, how to be humble, and how to appreciate life from a different perspective.

She also taught us about the importance of setting goals. Without a goal you have no direction. By working with Mom we were able to catch a vision for the type of homes we would eventually live in. We were able to study the families she worked for and take the best qualities we saw and apply them to our lives.

At the age of ten I had three goals that I wrote down on a small index card. My mom told me to keep the index card in my wallet so that as I'm going through life and if I start to detour, I will be reminded of what my goals are and stay on track. Looking at that index card would keep me from doing things that might not be good for my character or help achieve my destiny.

My first goal was to make my mother proud of me and for her to be happy about how I lived my life. Secondly, I wanted to graduate from college. No one from my family or my community had ever graduated from college. In my community, going to college was considered "square" and not popular, especially for someone like me who grew up poor. My third goal was to be able to earn enough money so that my mother would not have to work again. The way people treated her because she was a housekeeper saddened me; it was almost as if she was insignificant and did not exist. I achieved those goals and to this day I have that index card I wrote those goals on. On the other side I have my new goals that are drastically different and I am on my way to achieving them as well.

Having goals at the age of ten, staying with those goals, and accomplishing them step by step, one victory at a time, set me up to rise to the top!

Wright

I understand that something happened during your senior year in high school.

Luffborough

My senior year in high school was the turning point in my life. I had to decide if I was really going to pursue my goals or if I was going to give up on life. During my senior year in high school my family became homeless! My mom and my stepfather had been in an abusive relationship with each other and unfortunately the courts gave my dad our home. Mom had nothing in her name, so we had to leave. I was too old to go to a shelter. For six months of my senior year my brother and I were on the streets for most of that time.

It was then that I had to make the decision to either end my life or defy the hopeless future ahead of me. I had to decide if I had something inside of me that was greater than my current circumstance. I realized that being homeless was my moment of destiny—I was supposed to be homeless so I could get through this and then perhaps be a beacon of light or hope to other young people and families who find themselves homeless. I was so close to my dream of going to college that I actually looked at being homeless as a blessing—it was a way of being able to see the real needs of our society and being able to speak to them because I had walked in those shoes.

My passion to go to college was far greater than my pain of being homeless and I decided I wasn't going to give up—I was going to go for it and go to college. This meant I would have to do well in high school. Ironically, high school then became a safe haven for me—a refuge and a place to develop my potential. I learned to love school. I got involved with extra-curricular activities including basketball, student council, baseball, and choir. Other doors started to open and positive options started to appear in my life. Being involved in extra-curricular activities helped me stay out of trouble and develop other skills and talents I did not know I had.

Wright

How in the world did you overcome being homeless?

Luffborough

I worked hard academically, received support from a local educational opportunity center, and was admitted into college. My high school graduation was bittersweet because although I had nowhere to live, I had actually made it through. I also received an acceptance letter to Northeastern University in Boston, Massachusetts, and I was headed off to college. However, I didn't know what was going to happen to my family while I was gone—they were still on the streets. I had a brother still in high school, another brother in elementary school, and my mom soon gave birth to my sister. For me it was hard to be totally happy—although I was accepted into the college of my choice—the largest private university in New England—my family was still facing many hardships.

Wright

How did you get into college?

Luffborough

I did well in high school. During my freshman and sophomore years in high school I received B's and C's but during my junior and senior years I turned my grades around. When I was a junior I made the honor roll and during my senior year I got one B and all the rest were A's. This was because I had determined that school was my only ticket out of the life of poverty I was in. I had to excel. I took extra credit; I would come to school an hour early because I had nowhere else to go, and I became involved in every activity I could find because that was the only way I could see the light at the end of the tunnel.

I got into Northeastern University because of my grades and extra curricular activities. I even received some academic scholarships. Even though my circumstances seemed to be against me (being homeless with nowhere to go), I turned my situation around by getting an education.

I tell young people that they can turn their disadvantages into advantages, not only for themselves but also for other people.

When I was at Northeastern, at the end of the first semester of my freshman year, I earned a 2.0 grade point average—a C. From the viewpoint of the other students, their attitude was, "Well, you may want to 'C' yourself back down the freeway and go back home," because a 2.0 is not very good in college. What they didn't seem to understand was that six months before that 2.0, I was on the street, I had no home, and college was not even in my distant future. I had overcome a lot of obstacles to get there. I told them that because of my goals and the mindset I had at the age of ten I would set a new goal to raise my GPA each quarter and by the last semester of my senior year I would get a 4.0. Each semester my GPA increased and during my senior year in college I got a 3.9. Not bad for a formerly homeless kid.

Setting goals and sticking to those goals and making steady progress toward those goals always pays off.

Wright

What happened at your college graduation?

Luffborough

By the time I was a senior in college, I confronted all the demons I had been dealing with as a child. I planned to take them on head-on. One thing I wanted to do was overcome my fear of public speaking (as you recall I had a speech impediment in elementary school). I auditioned to be the student commencement speaker of my class at Northeastern. I auditioned with the valedictorians. At Northeastern you have to be a student leader to apply; it's not just for valedictorians, it's for any student who has a grade point average over a certain range, and for a student leader actively involved in the community and in the University. I accomplished all those things in college because of the foundation I'd had in high school.

Well, I won the competition! That same year then President Bill Clinton chose Northeastern to address the graduating class. That meant I, Doug Luffborough, would precede the President of the United States, Bill Clinton, as the student commencement speaker on national television! I would have the opportunity to thank my mom and to thank all those who supported me and other children in similar circumstances who have a dream to one day graduate from college. I would be able to see my dream come true on that day. I opened up my commencement address by singing a song as a way to calm me down (there were more than 14,000 people in attendance that day and several million viewers watching on national television—it was a live broadcast). Music was how I escaped as a child and it helped me with every area of my life.

I delivered my speech and it went very well. President Clinton was so impressed with my story and with me that he invited my mom and me to the White House. We spent three days in Washington, D.C., and the last day in the Oval Office with President Clinton. It was an awesome experience that reinforced my belief that if one sets a goal and has a dream and keeps going for it no matter what people say, no matter what circumstances dictate, it'll happen.

Someone once told me to never let someone's opinion of you become your reality, only you can dictate that. I was able to help more people than if I had given up. I think it's part of how I've risen to the top and why I believe that life is for the taking for those who aren't afraid to go after it. Let your legacy be told through the stories of the lives you have changed. Someone from your community, from your family, needs to rise up and be the example, why not you!

Wright
Where did you attend grad school?

Luffborough
After I finished Northeastern I decided I wanted to make a positive impact on young people in the world. In order to do that I needed to get my master's degree in education. I picked up a *U.S. News and World Report* magazine and read that the number one grad school for education in the world was Harvard University.

I have a younger brother who graduated from Lafayette College in Pennsylvania with a major in English and minor in pre-law. I told him, "Darrell, I have it in my heart that if we're really going to make a difference in this world we need to get our master's degrees." I told him that the number one school in the country at that time was Harvard University and that I really believed we should apply to that school. "I know we were homeless and our mom was a housekeeper," I said, "but I really believe that if one of us can get into Harvard, it will not only be a win for the family but it will be a win for a lot of people who are like us. It will be a win for people who have the potential but don't feel they belong at a place like Harvard. Let's just apply. What's the worst thing that could happen? At least we have the determination and the drive to apply to a school like Harvard. If they tell us no, then we know that school is not for us. But what if they tell us yes?" Well we decided to apply and on April 1, 1996, both of us were accepted into the Harvard Graduate School of Education. Remember that you have more power than you think! Even though we were homeless at one time in our life we were in fact Harvard material!

To my knowledge, we were the only two African-American brothers who had been admitted to the Harvard Graduate School of Education at the same time. We had the same major and took many of the same classes. My brother and I went through an accelerated ten-month program and graduated from Harvard in June of 1997.

I achieved those goals I had at the age of ten. I did well at Northeastern and was accepted at Harvard, so that goal was met.

My second goal was also met. If you could have seen the look on my mom's face when she was at the Harvard Yard—she was just beside herself. She told me, "I am just so proud of you. You exceeded every expectation I had. I just wanted you to do well. I wanted you to go to college and get a good job but you're also helping so many people. You have exceeded what I anticipated."

Wright

After attending Harvard, why Stanford?

Luffborough

I moved to San Diego, California, and started a nonprofit organization called Turning the Heart Center. Through the graduate school of business, Stanford has an executive program for nonprofit leaders called the Stanford Center for Social Innovations Fellowship Program. Since I was in the field of nonprofit management and wanted to continue making a difference in the lives of young people, I felt that having that extra credential from what many call "the Harvard of the West" would be a feather in my cap.

I applied to Stanford University and was accepted. I went through the fellowship program through the Graduate School of Business so that I could not only have more credentials, but also more credibility in my quest to make a difference in the lives of young people.

Wright

What helped you rise to the top?

Luffborough

There are several things that helped me. A primary resource was having a strong parent—my mother—who was also a mentor for me. Secondly was having a faith-based upbringing and having faith in God. If you think you can do it all by yourself, things will get very overwhelming. But if you believe in a higher power—something that is bigger than yourself—then you can let things go knowing that God is going to have things work out just fine. I use an acronym for the word P-O-W-E-R with the phrase "the P-O-W-E-R of Leadership." Each letter of the word POWER means something significant toward rising to the top:

P stands for "purpose-driven." I truly believe the reason I was able to rise to the top was because I found my purpose in life at an early age. Once people realize they have a purpose in life, they're not side-tracked by other social ills that can impact them—they stay focused and keep their eyes on the prize. When I speak to a lot of young people I ask them, "If money was no object and if you could do any-thing in this world, what would you do?" Unfortunately the most common response is, "Uh, I don't know"! That motivates me more and more to reach out to our nation's young people. If they don't know now, then what will they know ten years from now? That alarms me. I have two young children and I want them to grow up in a country that has people who aren't afraid to lead. They're going to know how to lead and then go out and do it.

Sometimes leadership is ugly but leadership is necessary. One as-pect of being a leader is being misunderstood. The one way to build leadership is by having people identify what their purpose is in life. Daily focus on your purpose gets you closer to your goals and aspira-tions. When you don't know what your purpose is, your life has no meaning and for the rest of your life you will continue to ask yourself two questions: who am I and why am I here?

O stands for "opportunity-chaser." Life isn't going to hit you in the head and say, "Hey, here's this million dollar opportunity for you, would you like to take advantage of it?" You're going to have to go out there and work for it. You have to chase opportunity—opportunity doesn't come to you, you have to go to it. I teach young people to look at their disadvantages as opportunities and I tell them about my experience of going from homeless to the White House, to Harvard, and then to Stanford. I tell them I took the situation of being homeless and turned it into an opportunity to get into college.

When the college's admissions office saw my application, they saw I didn't have an address (I had to put the address of the high school I attended). I told them, "I'm a formerly homeless teen but I believe that I'm college material and here's the reason why . . ." When I took advantage of that opportunity, I stood out among the other students.

From what I noticed while I was in college, most upper and middle class students took it for granted; but to me, going to college was a privilege and I treated it as a privilege. One example of this was when my brother and I were at Harvard. We were the first to arrive and the last to leave class. We asked for extra credit in all of our classes and wore shirts and ties to class. What you put into life is what you get back. Opportunities are right around the corner for those who are going after them. You have to ask yourself what gives you the competitive edge in life?

W stands for "willingness to go solo." I talk to young people about not being afraid to stand up for what they believe in—if they have a dream or a goal, step out and go for something they want more than anything. They need to hang around with people who lift them up and who don't bring them down. When I wanted to apply to college, many of my friends tried to discourage me. They thought I was trying to be bigger than I actually was and I had to distance myself from them. I realized that they're not living my dream and my unique qualities are totally different from their unique qualities. I decided that in order to reach my goal I couldn't be afraid to go solo.

Many young people live their lives watching their dreams being fulfilled through the lives of others with half the potential, half the skill set, half the education, half the home training, half the work ethic, and half the character; but because of negative influences and the people around them they have not been able to see the power and potential in their own lives. Therefore other people take what was intended for them. In order to go places other people aren't destined to go, you have to be willing to do the things other people aren't willing to do.

The E stands for "enthusiastic spirit." Those people in life who rise to the top are people who have a contagious spirit. Others want to be around them—they want to meet with them. In my life I always look at the glass as half full. I'm a person who believes that one's attitude does determine one's altitude and I always look at the positive side of any situation that happens in my life. When bad things happen to me I ask myself how can I turn it around? How can I use it for my advantage? An enthusiastic spirit will open the door to success. Usually when bad things happen people get upset, they wallow in it, and they're distressed. I'm not going to say I don't feel like doing that sometimes, but I look for the life within the terrible circumstance and how I can turn it around. An enthusiastic spirit is not something that school can teach you—you have to learn it by watching others who have risen to the top by going through it!

The R stands for "relationship-builder." In order to really rise to the top you have to be someone who is focused on building quality relationships with everyone you encounter. I truly believe that when we meet others and when other people come into our lives it's for a reason. They may be a part, maybe in a small way, of building your destiny, but you have to look at it that way.

Having this opportunity to meet with you and to be a part of this project is important to me because who knows what the future will be? My mentor and pastor, Sergio De La Mora, teaches that the people are always more important than the project. Most importantly, I want an opportunity to tell my story. I want an opportunity to inspire other people who may have been in my situation. Perhaps I can inspire those who have not been in my situation but who have a spirit of excellence inside them to always strive to be better in every area of their lives. When it comes to being an effective relationship builder, the greatest advice I was given was to learn the game of golf. The greatest deals in America are made on the golf course.

Wright

What's your next life goal?

Luffborough

My next life goal is to make a positive impact by turning the hearts of our nation's youth. I had an opportunity to develop youth programs in Hong Kong, Singapore, and Malaysia. What this has shown me is that human need and human interest has no boundaries—it's all across the globe. Young people are yearning for someone to teach them how to be better and to give them the love and encouragement they need to pursue their dreams.

My goal in the next five to ten years is to be able to go out and speak to different companies and universities across the United States and be able to share my testimony and raise money to be able to build nonprofit organizations like Turning the Hearts Centers throughout the nation. I want these centers to be a place where young people can find the leadership skills, the motivation, the inspiration, and most importantly the tools to be successful in their lives.

Wright

What a great conversation, Doug. I really appreciate your taking all this time with me today to talk about some things that are really important. I know that the readers of *Rising to the Top* are going to enjoy this as much as I have.

Today we've been talking with Doug Luffborough. Doug is CEO of Luffborough & Associates. He is also the founder and Chief Managing Consultant of a community-based nonprofit organization called Turning the Hearts Center, in which he empowers youth and family development.

Doug Luffborough

DOUG LUFFBOROUGH is a dynamic and powerful keynote speaker, trainer, and educational consultant. He brings over fifteen years of experience working with individuals and corporations to maximize their potential and reach their goals. Devoted to youth and family empowerment, Doug is also the Chief Managing Consultant for Turning the Hearts Center, a community-based, non-profit organization. The organization's mission is to turn the hearts of youth and families through education, leadership development, and family enhancement services. He holds a BS in business administration from Northeastern University, a master's degree from the Harvard University Graduate School of Education, and a fellowship for non-profit leaders through the Stanford University Graduate School of Business. Today he lives in Chula Vista, California, with his wife Claire and their two daughters, Makenna and Micaela.

Douglas E. Luffborough, III
Luffborough & Associates
Speaking, Training, and Consulting Services
1654 Picket Fence Drive
Chula Vista, CA 91915
Phone: 619.934.6718
E-mail: dougluff@yahoo.com
www.turningtheheartscenter.org

PRACTICAL SOLUTIONS TO HAPPY LIVING—EVERY DAY!

Joanie Winberg

"Our happiness depends on the habit of mind we cultivate.
So practice happy thinking every day.
Cultivate the merry heart, develop the happiness habit,
and life will become a continual feast."
—*Norman Vincent Peale*

Being happy is a choice you face every day of your life.

Is happiness and the feeling of gratitude what you feel on a daily basis or is stress and the feeling of being overwhelmed seem like a normal lifestyle? Has the feeling of stress become so familiar that you don't know any other way to live your life?

How do you break this mindset? What path do *you* choose?

If you're still struggling with the rough road, then it's important to figure out how to break the old mindset and get rid of the negative tapes or the thoughts that are not serving you—to break free of frustration and stress. We want you to strive for the "sigh of relief" feeling you get when you let go and learn to live a lifestyle of more ease, happiness, and fun.

The feeling of true happiness is a result of living your life based on your purpose—knowing why you were placed on this earth. We all have a purpose in life. For example, Mother Teresa's purpose was to work with the poorest of the poor in the slums of Calcutta—to love and care for those persons nobody was prepared or cared to look after. As the "Happy Wednesday Lady," my purpose is to be a joyous and glowing reflection of my soul while serving others to make a difference in the world—to empower people to be *happy*... to enjoy the journey of one's life.

As president of the Happy Wednesday Corporation, my commitment is to have every component of the corporation provide tools and techniques to help make happiness contagious—to bring more joy and the feeling of gratitude into a person's life as well as the world—*every day!*

For example, my mission as a speaker/trainer, business/life coach, radio personality, and a Certified Laughter Leader is to empower people to understand and believe in themselves, to help people rediscover the true magnificence that already exits within them, and to enjoy a feeling of contentment and happiness on a daily basis.

To keep the momentum going, *The Happy Wednesday Broadcast* was designed as a midweek *boost* to inspire people every Wednesday worldwide with inspirational quotes and tips. The mission of the program is to make Wednesday a "Power" day and banish "hump" day forever. The broadcast may be heard on 95.9 WATD-FM in Boston every Wednesday morning at 7:27 and 8:55 or can be received through your e-mail or downloaded to your iPod.

To reinforce this process of feeling happier on a daily basis, I created the *Happy Wednesday Broadcast 40 Days to a Happier Life* CD and journal set. These powerful tools will help transform stress into fun and ease in forty days or less for my clients, my audiences, and you, the readers, so that you can achieve an even higher level of contentment. The set includes two CDs and a unique instructional leather-bound journal. More details are on my Web site.

The fifth component of the Happy Wednesday Corporation was created because I wanted to make a difference in the world on an even larger scale. The non-profit Happy Wednesday Foundation was established to raise funds for organizations such as Habitat for Humanity, the organization that helps fulfill families' dreams of owning their own home.

To start your journey of happiness and the feeling of gratitude *every day,* follow these three practical steps:

Step #1—Ten minutes a day can lead to a happier you.

Having the privilege of coaching people worldwide, as well as conducting work/life balance workshops for business, universities, and parents' groups, I see a common theme—people forgetting to take care of themselves—lack of self-care.

During a work/life balance workshop I conducted for a university in Boston called "When Work/Life Balance Collide," I asked the women in the audience what they did to nurture themselves on a daily basis for at least ten to fifteen minutes. The majority said they do very little or nothing. One woman rolled her eyes and commented, "Who has time?"

Consider this: If you are not recharging your own batteries on a daily basis, how can you remain healthy both mentally and physically? How can you be the best you can be as a parent, partner, employee, or a boss?

Having been a single mom for twelve years, I have had to learn to take care of myself first. I remember in the beginning, someone said to me, "If you crumble, so will your children." Remembering the importance of being the best I could be for my children allowed me to feel less guilty when I did take time for myself.

This sage advice fits in any situation. Ask yourself, "In order to feel more energetic, who needs to be re-energized? Where does it have to start? How can I make a difference in the lives of others if I am not committed to taking care of myself first?"

Here are four self-care tips to help you feel more energetic and happier:

1. Make a commitment and give yourself permission to include yourself on your daily to-do list, even if for only ten minutes.
2. For an instant recharge (office or home), take three deep breaths—*really* deep breaths—with your eyes closed and exhale slowly. If possible, change the view. Get up and walk into a different room or step outside. While inhaling, use all your senses and focus on your surroundings. Focus as if you were going to paint, write, record, or describe to someone what you are feeling.
3. Include in your schedule a daily form of exercise. Be realistic! It's more important to be consistent. Start with baby steps.
4. Find a place where you can relax and let go of your worries and stress. If you enjoy being outside: garden, take a

walk, or enjoy the beach. If you prefer being indoors (office or home) you can choose among the following: Find a favorite chair, room, or even a corner of a room. Surround yourself with favorite pictures of friends or family, special mementoes, books, artwork. Create a place that feels right for you—it can be a physical place or a place in your mind where you can go for reflection and relaxation. The purpose is to allow yourself to connect to a special place and start to feel relaxed instantly.

Your mission is to defuse your stress, feel more energized, and enjoy the feeling of happiness. Keep it simple! There is no right or wrong; it's what works for you, your style, your needs, and your schedule. Do what you can do easily even if for only ten minutes.

Here are a few examples of how others have learned to feel more energetic and happier:

From a young couple with a new baby:
"My wife and I have been married two years and we just had our first baby four months ago. We both are entrepreneurs working from the same house and have quickly found that simply going through the day leaves us unfulfilled and feeling further apart. As speakers and coaches, we have begun to practice more of what we preach by taking control and creating choices that will lead us to the feelings we desire. Now, instead of getting through the day, we focus on what we get *from* the day. One simple solution was creating at least ten minutes every day where we are together—truly together—with nothing else to distract. In this sacred time and space we receive a deeper conversation, a sense of fulfillment, or a memorable moment that allows us to stay connected all day. It seemed so simple at first; however, we have learned that it is the simple things in life that work the best."— *Jeffrey St. Laurent, JSL Coaching.*

From a successful businesswoman:
"Gardenias are my favorite flower. They symbolize beauty, perfection, softness, good luck, resilience, purity, love, and gratitude. Yes, gratitude. At one time I was embroiled in the poverty trap and abusive relationships with men. Thankfully, I had an epiphany and realized that I wanted my life to count for something. I didn't want to be a victim any longer. I mustered the courage to brake the cycle of abuse. After dumping my abusive boyfriend and firing my boss, I

started my own business and became empowered as a woman. I became the master of my own life, married the man of my dreams, and bought my beautiful home with those spectacular gardenias smiling at me in the front yard.

"When I cut a velvety soft gardenia and place it in water, the fragrant perfume fills the room. This brings joy to all of my senses: smell, vision, and touch. When looking at my beautiful gardenias, I can't help but be grateful. I spend ten minutes a day smelling the gardenias, caressing my purring cats, and writing in my gratitude journal. I always write down at least five things that I'm grateful for. To find tranquility and your life's purpose, you may not need to look farther than your own front yard."—*Linda Hollander, The Wealthy Bag Lady.*

From a nurse practitioner:

Barbara Phillips has always been drawn to the beach to find a greater sense of peace. She says, "It's not hard when you grow up in the San Francisco. Even as a child, whenever anything happened in my life, my immediate need was to walk on the beach. I always felt safe, secure, and that everything would be okay if I could just get to the beach. When I worked in hospice we had a ritual where we held a 'circle' when someone died. It was a way to remember them and let them go. That never worked for me. I always went to the beach and let them 'go' with the outgoing tide. It was after this time I was really able to understand the power and sacredness of 'my beach.' I now travel to 'my beach' whenever I feel the need to get grounded again." —*Barbara Phillips, Founder of OlderWiserWomen, Inc. and co-host with Joanie Winberg of Balance and Wisdom, Internet Radio for Women.*

Step #2—Celebrate and treasure your talents and strengths within for true happiness.

There is the common phrase I hear from my clients worldwide that can be described or disguised in many ways, yet all mean the same thing: *"I'm not good enough."* Where did that belief come from? Were we born with that belief? When we were admired as a baby, did people say, *"This baby will grow up to be . . . not good enough for anyone or the world?"* How did we come to believe this about ourselves?

Over the years, have you acquired what I call "layers" of an onion? Have your "gold nuggets"—the unique gifts you were born with— become buried with layers? Can you even recognize your true gifts?

Maybe we gathered layers from what we may have seen as role models while growing up or by what others told us what we are "not" over the years. For example, if you had a dream for a certain occupation, you might have changed your mind if you heard, *"You don't want to do that, you don't have the experience"* or, *"You are not smart or talented enough."* When we heard that, how did that make us feel about ourselves? What beliefs were we starting to believe about ourselves? Often, when we hear these negative comments at a young age, it tears down our self-confidence even more. What role do we play as parents in building our children's confidence? Now multiply that over twenty to thirty to forty years and think about how many layers of that stinky onion you have acquired!

Realizing we are all born with "gold nuggets" is a hard concept for many people to believe about themselves. How can you start to dig and find those buried treasures of "gold nuggets" that already exist within you?

To believe in your magnificence, frame your thoughts using a positive affirmation by thinking in the first person singular and in the present tense. For example, think and say out loud, *"I am beautiful, I am a winner,"* or, *"I work hard toward my goals every day."* Do this exercise every morning for at least twenty-one days (it takes twenty-one days to break your old beliefs and habits) and watch what happens!

To rediscover your gold nuggets, let's first focus on the outside or the physical beauty of yourself. Look into a full length mirror and make a list of what you admire and love about yourself. I know, you can easily think of what you *don't* like, but try to focus on what you love. For example, your beautiful eyes or your nice smile, soft skin or pretty hair. Keep going and continue to build your list. Do not allow yourself to think of anything negative. I also suggest asking your friends and family about what they see as your gold nuggets. You might be surprised! Add these to your list.

Now turn your attention to your inner beauty. Reflect on your strengths and what value you bring to the table as a human being. You are unique!

Helping people understand themselves as well as others is my passion as a behavior specialist.

Before I could understand and appreciate the strengths and the uniqueness of my clients, those in my audiences, as well as my children, I had to understand myself first. Through this process, I have learned to recognize and appreciate my own strengths and qualities.

After understanding myself, I decided to test this communication process with my children. The results showed my children are opposites in their personality styles. My daughter is very organized and task-oriented, while my son is people-oriented and loves to have lots of fun. I realized that during the last twenty-three years, I had been using the same methods to communicate with and motivate both my children. Now I realize my son has to be motivated by having fun and my daughter through organization and detail. No wonder parenting feels like such a challenge!

I also showed the results to my children to help recognize each one's uniqueness and to show them how to support one another. My daughter said, "I can help him get organized," and my son said, "I can help her to lighten up," and as a mom, I said, "Oh, how I wish I'd had this knowledge twenty years ago! It would have made my role as a parent a lot easier." As Dr. Rohm of Personality Insights, Inc. says, "If I understand you and you understand me, doesn't it make sense that we can have a better relationship?"

Think about your strengths and qualities and add them to your list. Here are some questions to get you started: Are you a natural leader? Do you have a sense of humor and enable those around you to lighten up? Are you a nurturer and help others feel loved? Are you detail-focused and assist people in being more organized? Are you generous, patient, understanding, or kind?

Now compile your list of inner and outer qualities. Make several copies and keep one in your office, your car, and at home. Always keep a copy with you to remind yourself of how magnificent you are. What's the purpose of having a list with you at all times? It will help change those old tapes of your inner voice that frequently tell you how you are "not good enough"—you need to be reminded of all your gold nuggets. Have you ever noticed how that inner voice can kick in automatically when you have a bad or challenging day? It's amazing how fast we can dump on ourselves. No matter what kind of day you have had, your gold nuggets and unique gifts do not disappear! They are always with you! Your list will help you to remember.

Read your list several times a day or at least once a day to remind yourself of how great you already are and yes, you *are* good enough!

Keep reading it until you believe it. Allow yourself to see the shining gold within. It's already there!

Step #3—Energy management leads to a happier you.

Finding balance in both your personal and professional life can help you enjoy a greater sense of peace and happiness within. Yet this is a huge challenge today for most people. Our lives seem busier than ever with the feeling of a "fast-paced, get-stuff-done" type of lifestyle. For some people, stress and the feeling of being overwhelmed seem like a normal lifestyle. Although everything around you can contribute to the severity of your stress levels, stress is truly self-inflicted.

So how do you create a new paradigm for your life? How do you enjoy a greater sense of peace and create new feelings of happiness in your life every day?

To create a new paradigm, start by implementing these three steps into your life:

1. Be aware and recognize the stressful situation by noticing where it is showing up in your body. Do you have tension or aches and pains in your shoulders, neck, chest, or stomach? Pay attention to what your body is telling you. This is your red flag.

2. Accept the situation. It is what it is. Yes, life can be very challenging at times. Now ask yourself, *"Do I really want to continue feeling this way? If I keep feeling this way, will this make the situation better? How can I help myself?"*

3. Understand the Universal Law called the Law of Attraction. Maybe you have heard the expressions, "What you think about, you bring about" or, "The more attention you give to something, the more attention it will give to you."

To understand how the Law of Attraction works, recognize if you are having feelings (emotions) of low, negative energy or high, positive energy. Several examples of low energy are stress, negativity, fear, resentment, worry, despair, or a sense of lack (lack of time or money). High energy is the feeling of joy, abundance, happiness, gratitude, love, and compassion. Notice how you are feeling just by saying the low and high energy words. Which words disempower you? Which words empower you? Your emotions and feelings are a reflection of your thoughts. We have the power within ourselves to live our lives with the feelings of high energy by creating our own reality with our thoughts. It's a choice!

To help yourself shift and create a new paradigm, choose one or more of the methods below that work best for you. *(Note: Before choosing a method, first imagine yourself standing at the bottom of a set of stairs. The bottom of the stairs represents low energy and the top of the stairs high energy. As you help yourself shift to higher energy, see yourself starting to climb the stairs. Keep those positive thoughts coming—amp it up and continue climbing. Most importantly, don't forget to celebrate every step along the way.)*

Eight easy methods to create a new paradigm:

1. *Become present in the moment* by observing everything around you this very minute. Use all your senses. Put yesterday's worries and tomorrow's concerns aside and think about only the present moment! Take a deep breath and observe everything around you as if you had to describe it to someone over the phone.

   This method really helped one of my clients. She was feeling overwhelmed with the process of having to select an assisted living facility for her father as well as deal with the chaos of remodeling their home in order to put it on the market. When her stress level seemed unbearable, she would take time for herself by going outside for a change of scenery, even if for only ten minutes. Taking several deep breaths and focusing on her beautiful surroundings, such as the smell of the fresh air, the birds singing, and the warmth of the sunshine on her face, helped her face the challenging situation by feeling refreshed, re-energized, and more focused.

2. *Focus on what is working "right"* in the situation and build on that to help yourself shift. Yes, you may be facing a very challenging situation, yet try to find something that is working or feels right, no matter how small.

   Allow me to share a story with you. This past winter, after spending about five minutes with a new client, I started to notice a particular trend in her conversation. Her focus in life was very negative and she was consistently finding fault with friends and family. My mission was to help her shift her old thoughts of low energy to high energy. I asked her if *anything* was going right in her life at this time. There was nothing but silence on the phone and then I heard, "It doesn't feel like it."

To help her shift, I decided to talk about the weather. I described my snowy day with freezing temperatures in Boston and asked her about the weather conditions she was experiencing in Florida. She described a beautiful day with blue skies and a temperature of 78 degrees. I asked her if comparing the weather conditions caused her to think of something going right for her that day. Instead of hearing silence again, I heard a resounding "Yes!" To this day, whenever she is having a challenging day, she remembers our first coaching session to help herself shift to high energy by immediately focusing on the blue sky and the beautiful weather.

3. *Be grateful.* At the end of each day make a list of at least three things you are grateful for in your life. People tell me that they wake up in the morning as well as go to bed at night listening to the news. Yes, we all need to be informed, yet is the majority of the news positive or negative? I suggest shutting the television off before going to bed and make a list of everything you are grateful for that happened that day. Notice how quickly and easily you fall asleep.

4. *Keep on laughing.* Laughter and a sense of humor will not only help you feel better, it will help you instantly shift to high energy and diffuse a stressful situation. It also has many health benefits such as reducing your blood pressure and heart rate. It also strengthens your immune system. There is a statistic that reports children laugh about three hundred times a day and adults laugh only about fifteen times. Yikes! What happened? My motto as a Certified Laughter Leader is: learn to let go, lighten up, and have fun!

5. *Do an act of kindness.* Pay close attention to how you feel when you do something nice for another person. It's a win/win situation.

    Here's a great example: one of my friends used to pay the toll charge of a $1.00 for the person in the car behind him. He didn't know the person, he just wanted to do something nice. Hmmm! What a pleasant surprise. Who knows what a difference that might have made in the receiver's day or life, not to mention the giver?

6. *Go to your memory bank* and think of a previous fun time or experience in your life that could bring a smile to your face instantly. One of my client's favorite memories was a vacation on a cruise ship. She remembers feeling the warmth of the

sun while sunning herself on the deck and sipping a margarita. Ahh! What a great vision. Can you feel the shift, too? Keep amping it up! Think of another time of joy!

7. *Create a vision* of an ideal lifestyle filled with happiness and joy. What would it look like? Who are you with? What would you be doing? I suggest writing your thoughts and feelings in a journal to experience your vision at a cellular level. Now, take it one step further by asking yourself, "What am I willing to change in my life to make my vision a reality? Am I committed to making these changes?"

8. *Nourish your mind and spirit* on a continuous basis by feeding your mind with inspirational books and CDs. Our minds can be compared to a garden—negative thoughts feed the weeds and positive thoughts like fertilizer help the flowers bloom and flourish.

Can you feel the shift in your energy with the different method(s) you have chosen? Once again, take baby steps and be gentle with yourself. Before you know it, you will have shifted from low energy to high energy and everything in your life will start to fall into place with more ease. Discover how you have the power to attract the right people and the right situations into your life. Feel the flow! I suggest watching for evidence of all the "good stuff" in life that shows up by keeping track on a daily basis and writing in your journal.

Once again, I can't emphasize enough how important it is to celebrate every step along the way, no matter how small, by doing something special for yourself. For example, take a bath, buy yourself a little gift. For me, even though I don't eat dessert very often, going to a Dairy Queen to have a chocolate cone with chocolate dip is a big treat. (It must be that chocolate thing.)

In conclusion, when you implement the three practical steps by taking time for yourself, celebrating all your strengths and talents, and managing your energy, does it seem that the people or situations around you have changed in order for you to feel happier or in reality is it that *you* have changed? So, who has the power to feel his or her own joy and happiness? You do . . . *you be the chooser.*

If any of the three steps of "Practical Solutions to Happy Living Every Day" have inspired you, changed your life, or supported you in any way to live your life with more joy, happiness, and fun, then my dream of making a positive difference in your life and in the world has come true. I have lived my life on purpose!

Love and Light!

"Your success and happiness lie in you.
Resolve to keep happy, and your joy and you shall form
an invisible host against difficulties."

—*Helen Keller*

Joanie Winberg

As the Happy Wednesday Lady and president of the Happy Wednesday Corporation, Joanie Winberg's mission is to have every component of her corporation provide tools and techniques to help make happiness contagious by bringing more joy and the feeling of gratitude into a person's life as well as the world . . . every day! She accomplishes this as a speaker/trainer, business/personal coach, radio personality, and a Certified Laughter Leader. As part sounding board and part strategist, Joanie is specifically focused on you and your success. Her experience represents a diverse clientele from industries such as manufacturing, retail, health care, non-profit sector, high-tech, and education. Winberg comes from the retail background and has owned and operated a True Value Hardware business for eighteen years. She is a proud single mom of two children—Kristy, twenty-six, Doctor of Audiology, and Michael, twenty-three, a recent graduate of Bentley College.

Joanie Winberg
Phone: 508.947.2750
E-mail: jw@joanwinberg.com
www.HappyWednesday.com

CHAMPAGNE IN THE MORNING
RISING TO THE TOP BY COACHING
YOUR INNER MILLIONAIRE

June Davidson

I view life as one views climbing a mountain. There are paths where the journey will be a breeze—the road will be easy, and time will pass pleasantly. But more often than not, the pathway will be nonexistent, the going steep and hazardous. For every step you take forward, you will slide back two. But you need not make the journey alone; there are always others willing to help when the going is tough.

Life is an adventure, a journey to the mountaintop that will refine and mold your character and your personality. You will meet other climbers, some of whom will only be passersby, touching you briefly and without lasting impact. Others will offer a helping hand; sharing their God-given talents and insights, they will become lifelong friends or mentors. Through their influence you will be able to climb a little further along your journey. The higher you climb, however, the thinner the air becomes and the more difficult the pathway. Traveling companions fall away. It will be lonely at the top unless you have others with whom you can share the joys of accomplishment.

You must be vigilant in lending a helping hand as you go, reaching out to others along the way. It is a rare privilege to serve as a guide and mentor and you can justifiably take pride and pleasure in watching people change through your efforts.

⋠⋩

One of the traveling companions I met along my way is a man named Jim Rohn. Jim is a master at communicating—one of the best-known motivational speakers and authors on the circuit today. He is a true philosopher, a "modern-day Will Rogers" as termed by one of his admirers. Not given to the use of "two-bit" words, Jim conveys his messages in brief, easy to remember "Rohnisms."

Over the years Jim has become a trusted mentor; he has had a major impact on my life and my thought processes. I have changed my vocation from real estate entrepreneur to seminar leader, author, coach, and mentor. Through his influence my work now touches far more lives in a dynamic, ongoing, and constantly changing pattern.

Jim has been ably supported in his meteoric rise by April Moon, a long-time friend and business adviser. She has played a major role in his name becoming a "household word" in our country and abroad. April organized and successfully marketed his seminars, helping to plot the road map through virgin territory. She helped Jim set standards for what would become a major new industry.

To help better understand how Jim achieved his successes, a little more about April is in order. It seems that I have known the two of them forever, as I progressed from seminar attendee to ardent Rohn advocate and follower, becoming true friends with both him and April along this incredible and exciting journey.

April is a beautiful former model and actor, a truly elegant lady. Not only is she beautiful but she is charismatic, and all eyes are drawn to her when she enters a room. She is like the Rock of Gibraltar—steady and unwavering in her principles.

Not only does April give others a helping hand, she is there when the going gets tough, able to boost flagging spirits. She takes pride in the accomplishments of others and stands tall in her beliefs. She has received accolades and admiration from all who know Jim's "right hand."

April stands alone in one of her accomplishments, having been on the cover of *Guinness World Records* twice for her prowess in archery. She holds thirteen world records in flight shooting. Together, she and Jim are a formidable team, influencing many to become true champions along the way.

Jim Rohn continues to be my mentor and has taken a role in developing the American Seminar Leaders Association. Whenever his busy schedule brings him to Southern California, he frequently visits our seminars where he assumes the role of teacher. Because he so generously shares his time, he is able to reach down from his mountaintop to help others just beginning their journey. A favorite Rohnism of mine is, "If someone is going down the wrong road, he doesn't need motivation to speed him up. What he needs is education to turn him around."

As President of ASLA, we provide ongoing programs and certification for people interested in becoming seminar leaders. I became involved with ASLA through a long-time business partnership with Paul Karasik, a recognized seminar leader who founded the firm. We have developed an intensive training program and a home study course to improve platform skills, we have developed back-of-the room materials, and taught attendees how to write and market seminar books.

ASLA is also actively involved in one-on-one coaching of Certified Seminar Leaders to maximize their potential. Lifestyle coaching—a practice begun in the mid-nineties—is widely recognized as the growth industry of tomorrow. Coaching Firm International is an acknowledged leader in this field.

❧

A lot of mystery surrounds the term "life coach." A life coach is one who coaches around challenges of everyday living. At CFI, however, we believe coaches should be narrowly niched in accordance with their expertise and experience. Our life coaches are positioned into categories of relationship, parenting, purpose, recovery from incest, in the flow, self-esteem, and possibility.

CFI has different coaches for each category. For example, our Possibility Coaches are what society labels "disabled." We prefer to view this niche as one with possibilities, changing the way the disabled are perceived. Each of our coaches has faced life-changing challenges—from being in wheelchairs to blindness and deafness, from physical amputation to emotional amputation due to emotional issues. These leaders are truly outstanding, not only for what they are accomplishing in their own lives but in leading others to step out and assume their rightful role in society.

Can you visualize yourself as a double amputee? Who could you turn to for guidance since the pathway you previously traveled has come to an abrupt end? Why not choose someone who has been down this road, one who was educated in the school of hard knocks? That expertise and experience can have a major impact on your future.

Jim Rohn has this to say about lifestyle: "Lifestyle is the art of discovering ways to live uniquely. Let others lead small lives, but not you. Let others argue over small things, but not you. Let others cry over small hurts, but not you. Let others leave their future in someone else's hands, but not you."

We are currently training Possibility Coaches through a scholarship program. They are a great inspiration and are making a tremendous difference in the lives they touch. Rohn says, "We must learn to help those who deserve it, not just those who need it. Life responds to merit, not need."

What are your talents and what can you do to assist just one other person to change his or her lifestyle and to find the way?

The field of coaching has transformed untold lives since its inception in the early nineties and it continues to do so as more and more people discover its benefits. Coaching is nothing so much as deep inquiry into your current situation through questioning and other exercises. A specially trained coach can guide you, support you, and sometimes even exhort you to fill the gap from current reality to future desires. Through questions, exercises, and deep listening, a coach assists clients to master new skill-sets, accomplish long-held goals, and take leaps they wouldn't have the courage to attempt on their own.

Why hire a coach? It is just like asking, "Why would I hire a fitness trainer?" People hire a coach as a guide in seeking direction in making better choices, acknowledging and celebrating their life, to encourage them to excel in whatever is important, and for brainstorming possibilities. These are reasons enough to consider investing not only your time but your finances in igniting that spark of life that flickers within and is just waiting to reach its full potential.

Would you hire a fitness trainer with no experience—one who did not take care of his or her own physical self? Jim Rohn answers the question "Why hire a coach?" by saying, "You can not speak that which you do not know. You can not share that which you do not feel. You can not translate that which you do not have. And you can not give that which you do not possess. To give it and to share it and for it to be effective, you first need to have it. Good communication starts with good preparation."

This is why you should hire a coach qualified by training, experience, and expertise in the area in which you seek education. CFI coaches possess these qualities in abundance.

Some people view rising to the top as ascending the corporate ladder, others as breaking the glass ceiling to overcome the impossible. What does rising to the top—being at the top—mean to you? What is your definition of success? We have different visions for our dream lives, but odds are good that our visions have at least one thing in common—we desire financial security for our families and we want to help others, giving back to those less fortunate.

Haven't you fantasized about being a millionaire? Wouldn't it be nice to enjoy the freedom having such a net worth would give you? Think about it: You could live in your dream house, perhaps a mansion in an upscale part of the city, or a sprawling home on the beach. You could drive a luxury vehicle that purrs along the road and makes driving fun. You could travel to exotic lands, or perhaps start a foundation to fund the dreams of others. The world would be at your feet, and the greatest freedom of all—the freedom of being able to choose what to do with your time—will be yours. Can you feel the energy and excitement that being a millionaire creates within?

If so, good, because imagining yourself as a millionaire—what I call *embracing the millionaire within*—is an important step on your journey to becoming financially secure. My system, *Coaching the Millionaire Within*, teaches you to unleash your inner millionaire. Utilizing the principles of coaching, I take you through a step-by-step process to identify your current money belief systems, overcome obstacles and blocks, and power yourself down the millionaire highway. On this journey, self-discipline must become a constant companion. As Jim would say:

- "The least lack of discipline starts to erode our self-esteem."
- "Discipline is the bridge between goals and accomplishments."
- "One discipline always leads to another."

Let *Coaching the Millionaire Within* teach you how to release the millionaire within you and help you achieve your financial goals.

First, your current money baseline is identified—what your mindset about money revolves around. You may be perpetuating a scarcity mentality without even knowing it. You might be spending money as fast as you make it because of feelings locked inside. Or you may be refusing to acknowledge your current financial situation honestly because of deeply-held fears that no matter what you do, it will never be enough. The possibilities are endless. A life coach will help you recognize these beliefs and deal with them; he or she will help you reach the next milestone on the millionaire toll way.

Through coaching techniques we uncover the money negatives holding you back and then go through an incredibly effective process to find your "programmers." Programmers are those people whose words about money have become embedded in your consciousness. After clearing away these unconscious beliefs, you'll be ready to start embracing your millionaire within. It doesn't matter what your current financial situation is. You can be in terrible debt and see no way out, you can be making a good salary and want to make the leap to great, you can be looking for a way to go from the workaday world of the wage slave to being more in control of your financial destiny. Whatever your current status, our system will assist in your millionaire quest.

Another Rohnism which bears repeating is, "We all know a variety of ways to make a living. What's even more fascinating is figuring out ways to make a fortune."

But before any of this can occur, you must catch the vision and believe it can *happen*. To begin with, I'm going to guide you to embrace your inner millionaire. What do I hear you saying? You don't have an inner millionaire? Let's get one thing clear—you *do* have an inner millionaire! It resides deep inside, just waiting to be discovered and come to the fore. You must allow it to take center stage in the Theater of the Mind.

The Theater of the Mind is my term for our internal dramas. We all have a theater within, complete with stage, actors, directors, and producers. In the *Coaching the Millionaire Within* process, we convince the directors and producers of the Theater of the Mind to cast you in a starring role on stage after you have rewritten the script.

The mind is our theater. Keep it cleared, clean, and inviting. The stage awaits your presence to share new ideas, concepts, extraordinary love, and all things possible. Step into your greatness on center stage for the incredible life, the drama, and comedy that you desire. There are no failures—it is the performance of your learning lessons and feedback. Accept it as that, take action and move forward. You transmit every opinion and belief to your subconscious through the Theater of the Mind. Using coaching principles, we can teach your subconscious a new role—that of starring in your own millionaire lifestyle. A choice Rohnism: "Don't spend most of your time on the voices that don't count. Tune out the shallow voices so you will have more time to tune in the valuable ones."

Another concept I talk about often on a personal basis with clients and in seminars is the idea of the One Cell. Within each of us resides the One Cell. It is the mother lode of all knowledge—the source of all wisdom. We are filled with the knowledge of all time—the wisdom of the ancients. Since we each own one of these treasure troves, I call it the One Cell/One Self. In Transcendental Meditation, we talk about touching the purity of who we are, of going back to the purity of our essence as a baby. The information and exercises are designed to help you learn to access the wisdom of the One Cell/One Self and activate it to create your millions.

Jim Rohn speaks often about his mentor and credits the importance of developing a life plan through his guidance—a plan that was instrumental in releasing his inner millionaire. He said, "I remember saying to my mentor, 'If I had more money, I would have a better plan.' He quickly responded, 'I would suggest that if you had a better plan, you would have more money.' You see, it's not the amount that counts; it's the plan that counts."

The other philosophy that has guided my efforts is one espoused by Native Americans. I am one-eighth Choctaw and have long studied native philosophies. One of the fundamental beliefs is that the One Cell/One Self is a pure essence buried deep within the soul. Another aspect deals with the mind. But who or what directs the mind? And why does it not always act in accordance with our higher good in a way that our One Cell/One Self might condone? That is the work of the Spirit, which tells us what it thinks we should do, regardless of the dictates of the mind or soul. I envision mine as an impish little angel, halo askew, who whispers directions that are often in my best interests to ignore. We can direct the mind to follow the dictates of the One Cell and ignore the distractions of the Spirit.

The One Cell/One Self defines our values. We must direct our minds to act with behaviors that uphold those values and learn to ignore the distractions of the Spirit. This is especially important when it comes to money. There is no virtue in being poor. Wallace Wattles addressed this in a classic work written seventy-plus years ago called, *The Science of Getting Rich*, and everything that he wrote then still holds true today. We have developed new technology and are far more sophisticated in our information delivery systems, but the laws of the universe do not change. This knowledge, combined with the art of coaching, enables us to harness these unchanging principles and apply them in our lives.

❧

Don't waste time worrying whether or not it is ethical to get rich. As long as you conduct yourself in a forthright and honest manner and don't step on or kick people on the way to success, the road is wide open. This may be a block you have to deal with in the clearing process. Set it aside and prepare to enjoy the ride. We're going to have some fun creating your own millionaire—designing your new lifestyle and declaring to the universe that this is your intention.

You need to acknowledge this daily and verbalize to those around you—"I'm going to be a millionaire." You might feel reluctant to declare such a thing. Why? Because you are afraid—afraid it won't happen, afraid you won't become a millionaire or even anywhere close, afraid you will be laughed at. But that very fear is part of your resistance—an obstacle to unleashing the power of your inner millionaire. If it was really important and you believed in the millionaire within, wouldn't you dare to say it out loud?

As Wattles says, "There is nothing wrong in wanting to get rich. The desire for riches is really the desire for a richer, fuller, and more abundant life—and that desire is praiseworthy. The person who does not desire to live more abundantly is abnormal, and so the person who does not desire to have money enough to buy all he wants is abnormal."

This is the attitude you need to assume along with the principles and philosophy of Jim Rohn. Get a good mentor and coach.

Jim, April, and I were on a trip to Las Vegas where we met T. Harv Eker. Harv is a mover and shaker and has impacted the lives of thousands with his books, his Millionaire Mind Intensive programs, and other training programs. On this trip, Jim was driving and I sat in the back, completing a series of coaching success tracts for people using Harv's programs. I bounced ideas off both Jim and April and in the process they became interested in this emerging industry.

On the return trip, we got into a discussion of coaching. Jim had just returned from a visit with his friend, Bill Bailey, and had sat in his office while he was coaching. Now thoroughly intrigued with the principles behind this, he made an offer I could not refuse. Once every six months he would group coach my PBCs (persons being coached).

His advice to the PBCs about the value of setting goals early in the program has a major impact; his shared wisdom and encouragement are invaluable in the learning process. Jim has this to say about goals: "Goals. There's no telling what you can do when you get inspired by them. There's no telling what you can do when you believe in them. And there's no telling what will happen when you act upon them." This is the man—Jim Rohn—who graciously extends a helping hand to others along the way.

Since creating your own millionaire is the first step to assuming it, let's get started! Money has a flow and energy of its own. If that flow is blocked by thoughts or beliefs, it will dry up. You won't be able to access the millionaire high road. The best way to get going on that millionaire journey is to assume a millionaire personality.

❧ ❧

Let me give you an example. I am fortunate to live in my dream house. Perched on the side of the San Gabriel Mountains near the end of a winding road so narrow that if you meet another car you have to back up, it offers views of the entire Los Angeles basin. I feed deer and raccoons and squirrels and birds from my balcony. My home is a safe harbor for my soul and I love it dearly.

The first time I walked into this house I knew it was mine! The problem was that I didn't have the money for the down payment or the means for financing. But here's the key concept: the minute I walked into that house I took ownership of it. I knew it was mine, and I knew some way would open for me to get the necessary funds. Within thirty days I earned the money for the down payment. That is the power of taking ownership, and taking ownership of your millionaire personality will activate the power of prosperity within you.

Now it's *your* turn to create ownership. Start by pondering what it is that you want in life. The first step to owning a millionaire lifestyle is to create one. How will you spend the riches? A new house, clothing and jewelry, or broaden your life through travel, lectures? Will you become a collector of paintings, rare books, or vintage cars? Do you want to own a boat, or buy good golf clubs? Or do you desire riches to help loved ones and others less fortunate? Will you take an active role in wiping out certain diseases?

❧ ❧

Sit down and savor the process of acknowledging what is important, what you really want in life. In the words of Thomas Edison, "All achievement and earned riches have their start in an idea." Make a list and update it often, deleting or adding as your heart dictates. Schedule time daily to work with your desires; never say you don't have time for this! Becoming a millionaire takes time, commitment, and passion. Can't you spare some time every day to make your dream a reality?

For the first session, give yourself thirty minutes to an hour. Sit down and brainstorm every single thing you want in life, from the smallest and most trivial to the biggest and wildest things imaginable. Write down abstract concepts such as love and intimacy; write concretes such as a new watch, or the latest best-selling novel by your favorite author. What about a new refrigerator for your parents? What about funding a church project or making a sizable donation to cancer research?

After your initial session, add to the list daily, or at least twice weekly. Once you've started this process you'll be amazed at how many things flow into your consciousness. Driving to work in the morning you'll recognize the Ferrari next to you as the car of your dreams. You will have the ability to make the purchase without the concern of how to pay for it. Don't throw out the baby with the bath water but do throw out the mentality of "I can't do this!"

Acknowledging your One Cell/One Self desires brings them to the fore where you can take action to add to your millionaire lifestyle. You are truly the star of the Theater of the Mind, instead of the bit part you have been playing.

Wattles calls this process conveying the "impression of increase," and he says it is what everyone is seeking: "The desire for increase is inherent in all nature; it is the fundamental impulse of the universe. People are seeking more food, more clothes, better shelter, more luxury, more beauty, more knowledge, more pleasure—increase in something, more life."

Jim Rohn's principles in *The Challenge to Succeed* identify the road map of how nature works to bring about increases in our lives. We are training people to teach these simplistic concepts with all proceeds going to International Education Institute, a nonprofit organization.

Jim's theory is you must plant in the spring. You weed the garden in the summer. Weeds are challenges in life; they are not something you handle—they are something you devastate. In the fall you can expect a good harvest. The winter is the hard time when you must begin all over again—you must prepare to plant in the spring.

Jim says, "You must get good at one of two things—sowing in the spring or begging in the fall." In order to have the increases you seek, you must prepare over and over again to diligently sow your seeds in the springtime.

❦

You have acknowledged your desires and that you are worthy to become a millionaire; now you must take an active step of faith which I call the visualization process. Make a vision board where you post pictures of your desires. This can be as simple or as complex as you wish, just remember that presentation is not nearly as important as proximity. The visualization process and the important role it plays are discussed at length in my book, *Coaching the Millionaire Within.*

And now there is one more task to add to your repertoire of millionaire envisioning. The final task is to take action.

Nothing activates the millionaire mindset better than taking action. Jim Rohn says it simply: "To become financially independent you must turn part of your income into capital; turn capital into enterprise; turn enterprise into profit; turn profit into investment; and turn investment into financial independence."

And so, take action! Make it fun and festive. Go to the dealership that sells the car of your dreams; take a test drive. Discuss the features of this model with the salesperson. Feel the richness of the leather seats; inhale that new car smell. Admire its maneuverability as you round a corner.

Or check out open houses until you find your dream home. Notice every detail—the crown moldings, the view from the backyard. How wonderful it would be to sit on the deck and enjoy nature every evening. How does it feel to live here? What do you think when you pull into the driveway and gaze at this special place you call home? Does it make your heart sing?

❦

Let me share with you one of my personal millionaire lifestyle tidbits. Here it is: Champagne in the morning. I love champagne. I have a shelf in my refrigerator dedicated to chilling champagne and the proper glasses. This is definitely part of my millionaire mindset! I believe that no occasion is too small that can't be better enjoyed with good friends and champagne. Life is an adventure, a wonderful outing to savor and enjoy. Long ago I envisioned that champagne—even in the morning, if I so desired—was an important part of my millionaire lifestyle.

Champagne in the morning lifestyle also speaks to something else in which I believe passionately—the need to celebrate. Part of standing tall in your new mental millionaire status is celebrating you. Commit to another visioning session and make a list of all the ways you most like to celebrate. Do you want a cold beer after you've finished a difficult project? Do you enjoy dining out and sharing a bottle of fine wine, or cooking dinner for friends and family? Does taking a drive in the country or going for a hike make you feel good? Make a list of all the things you like to celebrate and then do them. You've worked hard on embracing your inner millionaire—it's time to reward yourself! Choose something from your list and do it. And while you are off shopping, or bird-watching, or cooking, don't forget to feel the satisfaction of a job well done. Enjoy the knowledge that you are actively activating your millionaire mindset.

You have now gathered many components of the prosperous lifestyle you plan to enjoy. You have made a list of things you desire, you've created a vision board. You have actually gone out in the world to allow the millionaire within to take center stage.

Beware of the negative thoughts that will creep in such as "you're broke; you will never be able to buy that home you want." Turn the negatives into positives since doubt can actually be good. It pinpoints areas that you don't actually believe can happen. Bring doubt into the open and deal with it positively so that it does not block your inner desires. You can face the future with apprehension or you can welcome it with anticipation. There are two choices—either make a living or design a life.

❧❧

Now that you're excited and can feel the energy generated by embracing your inner millionaire, let's ponder some practicalities. You've caught the spirit and you feel the intent to become a millionaire in the innermost core of your being. How are you going to accomplish it?

Wattles reminds us to do everything with the firm conviction that we are advancing personally and that our advancement benefits others—we can hire someone to help with the housework so our time is used to its best advantage. By benefiting others on your journey to becoming a millionaire, you are sharing the wealth as you go.

It is not my intent to give you specific financial or business advice. There are many fine books and programs on the market to serve as your guide in this. What I want to emphasize is the underlying aspect of choosing to believe in your self-worth enough to activate your millionaire status. As you begin to embrace your inner millionaire, you will have difficult choices to make. This will happen naturally—you can't begin a powerful process such as this one without changes resulting. And it doesn't matter where you are now, you *can* get there from here. Wallace Wattles has this to say about getting rich: "No matter whether you are a physician, a teacher, or a clergyman, if you can give increase of life to others and make them sensible of the fact, they will be attracted to you, and you will get rich."

Once you've activated your inner millionaire, the stage is set. As long as you pay attention regularly and follow the exercises, the millionaire mindset will not disappear. Much like releasing the genie from the bottle, your inner millionaire is here to stay as long as you coddle and delight him with constant attention. The focus of your attention will become manifest in your life. The Law of Attraction is one of the fixed laws of the universe, so use it to your benefit.

Write out an action plan; list the specific steps you will take to increase earnings. How will you arrive at your millionaire status? Begin by identifying the goals, recognizing blocks and obstacles, and then brainstorming ways around them. Focus your mind on what you want to attract into your life, not on the negatives you want out of it. If you find this process difficult, you may want to consider hiring a coach to assist.

Jim Rohn has this to say about the power of personal development:

- "Unless you change how you are, you will always have what you've got."
- "We can have more than we've got because we can become more than we are."
- "Success is neither magical nor mysterious. Success is the natural consequence of consistently applying basic fundamentals."
- "Pity the man who inherits a million dollars and who isn't a millionaire. Here's what would be pitiful: If your income grew and you didn't."

Activate that millionaire within today! *You do have a choice!*

Finally, and most importantly, have an attitude of gratitude. Your One Cell/One Self is a deeply grateful entity. Let this attribute fill you in a conscious manner, so that you are a being of thankfulness for all you have achieved and will continue to achieve. Gratitude is pure focus on what we love and appreciate in our lives and concentrating on that which we love will bring us more of it.

Maintain your focus on what you desire, be grateful as you learn to embrace your inner millionaire. Begin now to enjoy the life of your dreams! Reach out to others and share the wealth you possess, give freely of yourself and your finances. Assume the role of your dreams—become the star in your life and play to SRO crowds, consistently on center stage.

Throughout this chapter, I have chosen to honor my good friend and mentor, Jim Rohn, and have quoted extensively from *The Treasury of Quotes.* He is a master motivator, an outstanding communicator, a leader who willingly gives of his time and wealth to help others reach their potential. The influence he has had on my teaching and coaching styles is evident.

If there is worth and merit within this chapter, part of the credit goes to Jim, a good man, and an inspiration to all with whom he comes in contact. Truly, "sharing makes you bigger than you are" and "the more you pour out, the more life will be able to pour in."

June Davidson

JUNE DAVIDSON is a master certified action coach, certified seminar leader, trainer, public speaker, and author. She is President of the *American Seminar Leaders Association (ASLA)*, one of the fastest growing national training and certification programs for coaches, seminar leaders, and authors.

Nationally acclaimed Coach Instructor and Mentor for professional coaches, June Davidson won first place award in the Category of Education at the Invention Convention presenting the ASLA's accredited training courses.

The author of over twenty continuing education courses approved by California Department of Real Estate, Board of Behavioral Science, Board for Certified Public Accountants, California State Bar, and MCLE. She has also written a book and seminar series *Financial and Lifestyle Protection*. She has an innate ability to bring out the best in the coaches in all phases of coaching practice.

Her current book, *Marketing Your Coaching Practice with Seminars* was published December 1, 2004.

An experienced radio talk show host, June Davidson co-hosted two shows for Los Angeles KIEV AM radio and advocacy program for the grassroots coalition *Citizens Against Lawsuit Abuse* and *Publicity Hounds*. She has been on numerous television shows including Phil Donohue.

Initially working in marketing and selling ASLA's innovative educational products, she became a seminar leader and coach after she developed courses for the real estate industry. She created a specialized niche, making presentations to real estate professionals from Vancouver to Mexico.

June Davidson
2405 E. Washington Blvd.
Pasadena, CA. 91104
Phone: 626.791.1211
E-mail: info@asla.com
www.asla.com

TWELVE FACETS OF BEING A SUCCESSFUL LEADERSHIP SHERPA^SM COACH

Jennifer Mounce

The old buzz words around employee empowerment and satisfaction still ring true for many companies. Leaders talk of creating an empowered workforce. Managers are measured on employee satisfaction. There are many companies out there that talk a good game but never deliver on their message. The companies that seem to be "getting it right" are bringing coaching into their cultures. The art of coaching as a part of leading your team is becoming a critical leadership ability. A study was commissioned by a Fortune 500 company with MetrixGlobal in 2002 to determine the business benefits and return on investment for an executive coaching program. The study showed that coaching produced a 529 percent return on investment and significant intangible benefits to the business. Overall, productivity (60 percent favorable) and employee satisfaction (53 percent) were cited as the most significantly impacted by the coaching. Respondents defined productivity in this context as relating to their personal or to their work group productivity and half (50 percent) documented annualized financial benefits. Employee satisfaction was viewed both in terms of the respondents being personally more satisfied as a result of the coaching as well as the being able to increase the employee satisfaction of their team members.[1]

---

[1] Source: *Executive Briefing: Case Study on the Return on Investment of Executive Coaching,* MetrixGlobal, LLC, http://www.metrixglobal.net.

The manager as coach and employee as coachee relationship should not be taken lightly. It takes skill to be a coach, particularly a Leadership Sherpa[SM] Coach. Coaching is about two individuals connecting to fully support one of the individuals in reaching desired goals. This is not unlike the Nepalese Sherpas who connect with Western mountain climbers to support them in reaching their desired goals such as summiting Mt. Everest.

Like the native Nepalese Sherpas who are expert mountain climbers, guiding mountaineers up peaks like Mt. Everest, Leadership Sherpa[SM] Coaches guide their coachees to stay focused on their goals and ensure they have the tools and resources needed to reach their peak. In order to rise to the top as a leader you must be able to coach your team to get to the top as well. The term "Sherpa" is meant to insinuate many things about how you coach. As a Leadership Sherpa[SM] Coach you are: an expert, a guide, a resource, and a motivator just to name some.

Coaching is a skill that can be learned, as can creating a coaching culture. While you may not be able to learn everything there is to know about coaching in this one chapter, you can expect to understand some key coaching concepts. The rest of this chapter will introduce you to the twelve facets of Leadership Sherpa[SM] Coaching. What this chapter may very well do is wet your appetite for a deeper understanding of how coaching skills can assist you and your team in creating an empowered and satisfied workforce. All of these skills, when put to use correctly, add up to a more empowered and satisfied workforce.

The twelve facets are divided into four key areas: Relating, Empowering, Designing, and Guiding. All of the facets are imperative to a successful journey for the coachee. As a Leadership Sherpa[SM] Coach, visualize the employee's goals being at the top of a summit. As the coach and coachee first begin the coaching process, information is being exchanged both ways. The coach and coachee are establishing their relationship and must get to know each other and feel comfortable in a coaching relationship. This is foundational to the rest of the coaching process. As the coachee begins his or her journey, the coach will advise, recommend, and acquaint the coachee with tools, resources, and ideas that will assist in keeping him or her moving forward. Along the way, the coach and coachee will cooperate with one another. They will collaborate as they strategize the design of the next goal or the best way to accomplish the goal at hand. As the coachee continues along on his or her journey, the coach will provide the support, motivation, and necessary challenges to empower the coachee to succeed. Let's explore each key area, specifically, the twelve facets of Leadership Sherpa℠ Coaching in more detail.

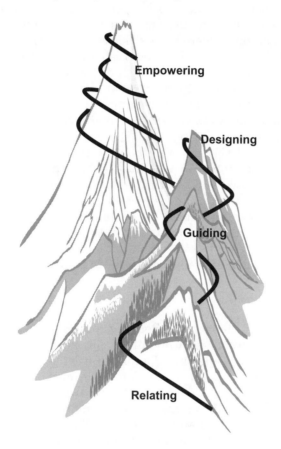

Relating

This area is comprised of three facets: Connecting, Listening, and Questioning. Relating is a foundational element on which the other three areas can develop. The facets within Relating allow for bonding and rapport to take place between coach and coachee.

1. Connecting—As the coach and employee connect and get to know each other, they are establishing trust and respect. Just because someone works for you doesn't mean you automatically have that person's trust. Establishing a coaching relationship with the in-

dividual is one way to help establish and gain trust. Being able to connect takes some ability to be flexible in your own communication style and understand what style the employee you are coaching will be most receptive to. Connection happens by being curious, putting judgments aside, taking genuine interest in the person, and actively working to understand where he or she is coming from.

2. Questioning—Questioning and Listening are both techniques you can use to fully connect with each other. Take the time to ask questions of your coachees. Find out what motivates them, what gets them excited, what de-motivates them, how they like to be recognized for their accomplishments, what their career goals are, and what you can do to support their success.

3. Listening—Actively listen to the answers provided to you. This is an exchange of information because as you ask questions—you don't just want answers in return, you want to fully hear those answers. Truly understand what the coachee is saying to you. If you are uncertain, ask more questions. If you find yourself assuming, ask more questions. Part of listening is to give the coachee your undivided attention when you are together. Shut off e-mail, the phones, instant messaging, the radio, and anything else that could create a distraction for you.

Guiding

As you build on the facets of Relating, you may move to Guiding. This next group consists of: Acquainting, Advising, and Recommending. Part of being a Leadership Sherpa[SM] Coach is knowing when to share your wisdom, knowledge, and tools to support the coachee's journey and when it is more powerful to empower the coachee to find the answers on his or her own. Guiding conjures up an image of a flexible rope on one side of an obscure path. The coachee doesn't have to hang on for dear life, but has the comfort of knowing the rope will be there to help find the path again if it becomes unclear.

4. Acquainting—A good Leadership Sherpa[SM] Coach will provide the coachee that sense of security without directing or forcing the coachee in a particular direction. One way to guide coachees is by acquainting them with the concepts and tools they can use to find the right path. "Acquainting" is giving them an introduction to something they weren't familiar with prior to making the acquaintance.

Here's a scenario that will be used throughout this facet to provide examples and to also establish the subtle distinctions between each facet. Your coachee is tasked with leading a new project for the company. While you have some knowledge in this project area from work at your last employer, this is a completely new area to your current company. Part of the project will be to identify a software application to utilize. As a coach you may acquaint your coachee, Jim, with the capabilities of some of the software on the market today by sharing a couple of articles you've seen recently in a trade journal.

5. Advising—Leadership Sherpa^SM Coaches may advise on things they have done before or where they know the path is good or a particular path to avoid. Coachees can choose to use or ignore the advice as a part of the coaching process. Let's take our project scenario above as an example. Since you had worked on a similar project at a different company, you may advise Jim to keep his eye on two of the deliverables. Based on past experience you know they can come up fast and will quickly delay the whole project. Your coachee, Jim, may or may not heed your advice, but it is part of providing the tools and resources to assist him in accomplishing his goals.

6. Recommending—This is the third facet. A recommendation might be made to show a coachee an option he or she was not seeing on his or her own. For instance, let's use our project example one more time. As a Leadership Sherpa^SM Coach, you know through conversations with Jim that he is headed down a path with identifying a software application that will support the project. While all of the applications on the table seem appropriate, you saw an ad recently on similar software and recommend to Jim to take a look at it as well.

Here are the subtle distinctions between the three facets: You might *acquaint* if you were already familiar with a software application and knew where to go find out about it, or had some information on it already that you could share. You may *advise* if you had experience, good or bad, in working with the firm that makes the software application. Lastly, you might *recommend* when you are not familiar enough yourself to acquaint or advise, but see an option or alternative solution that Jim is unaware exists.

Designing

As the coaching continues there will be an opportunity to design. As a manager and leader of your team it is much more powerful to collaborate, strategize, and cooperate with your teammates to establish their goals than to dictate them. This is the key area of designing.

7. Collaborating—Part of goal-setting is collaborating on ideas. Your employees may share their career vision with you. You in turn

may share your career vision for them and discuss where the two visions align. Collaborating is a process by which you and your employees exchange ideas and information to co-create the end result.

8. Strategizing—You may also strategize together on how to make the goals a reality or on a plan that allows employees the opportunity to move in the direction that aligns with their long-term career goals. Another facet of designing is cooperating. Both you and each of your employees must be willing to cooperate with each other in order to design goals you both find agreeable.

9. Cooperating—Cooperation is hinged on finding a win-win solution. This co-creation allows the employee to develop and supports them in taking ownership of his or her goals.

Empowering

Empowering is the final key area in our review of the four key areas and twelve facets to Leadership Sherpa[SM] Coaching. Empowering is typically a more effective part of coaching for managers after there is a rapport established and the paths (goals) are designed. You may or may not be guiding before you empower. The three facets of empowering are: Motivating, Supporting, and Challenging.

10. Motivating—Motivating is a powerful coaching tool. As you relate, find out what serves to motivate and de-motivate each of your employees. It is important to remember that what motivates you may not motivate them. Put yourself in the shoes of each employee.

11. Supporting—Support is another big piece of the success indicators. If an employee feels supported in his or her work toward achieving established goals, that employee is more likely to succeed.

12. Challenging—Part of empowering is also to challenge the employee. You may challenge the employee to:

- Do his or her absolute best.
- Do better than he or she did last time.
- Try something he or she has never done before.

Your challenges as a leader and manager are critical to assisting your employees in their growth and development process. Do not be afraid to challenge your employees a little more than they may challenge themselves. Coupled with supporting and motivating, employees may feel up to the challenge. You will have empowered them to succeed.

The four key areas and all twelve facets of Leadership Sherpa^{SM} Coaching create a framework that allows your employees to flourish. It gives an opportunity for the employees to take ownership in designing their future outcome. All of the elements of Leadership Sherpa^{SM} Coaching steer clear of creating mandates or giving directives. Coaching serves to grow and develop employees by allowing them to seek out their paths and work toward achieving their goals knowing that you are there when they need support or guidance. On one side, you may ask just the right questions through relating and designing for them to realize an answer on their own. On the other side, you may guide by making a recommendation that saves them weeks of headaches.

Knowing just how and when to intertwine Relating, Guiding, Designing, and Empowering is what makes a successful Leadership Sherpa^{SM} Coach. What do you need to do in order to become a Leadership Sherpa^{SM} Coach for your employees? My recommendation is that you ask powerful questions and listen actively to your employees' responses. Your challenge is to take the time to collaborate on each employee's goals. You can empower yourself to become a successful Leadership Sherpa^{SM} Coach!

Jennifer Mounce

JENNIFER MOUNCE is the original Leadership Sherpa^{SM} Coach and founder of Coach Effect, a leadership and organizational effectiveness boutique in Chicago. Jennifer is a published author, speaker, and she hosts a podcast program: The Leadership Sherpa^{SM} Channel. Fourteen years of corporate experience include organizational development, coaching, communications, and training. Some of the organizations Jennifer has supported include: Motorola, Harris Bank, Doubletree Hotel & Resort, and Foote, Cone & Belding. Jennifer is a graduate of Coach University. She received her bachelor's degree in Speech Communication from the University of Illinois, her master's degree in Human Resource Management from Loyola University Chicago, and is a certified Senior Professional in Human Resources.

Jennifer Mounce, SPHR
Coach Effect, LLC
Chicago, Illinois
Phone: 773.580.8360
www.coacheffect.com

LIVING AT FULL CAPACITY

Dan McArthur

"There lies within each person, a capacity to better understand limitations, commit to authentic change, and live in fuller realization of purpose, potential, and destiny."

There lies within each person a capacity . . .

I will never forget the shock and concern I felt on that warm spring day in Riverside, California, when I walked out in the driveway and found my first mentor on my incredibly fast Suzuki 1100 motorcycle, planning to go for a ride. He could see the look on my face and hear the surprise in my voice when I said, "Randy, what do you think you are doing?"

After all Randy had done for me to help me integrate into student leadership my first year of college life, you would think that I would be glad to let Randy go for a spin . . . but I wasn't! He had been helping this eighteen-year-old know-it-all learn how to overcome my deep sense of insecurity and the self-doubt I had so skillfully hidden from most onlookers. During times when I felt overwhelmed by my role in campus leadership, Randy helped me identify my inner potential and the lessons from my past that I so easily overlooked. At times when I wanted to quit, he encouraged me to try again.

Randy had a huge heart and he had courageously cultivated his own ability to overcome and press on when things looked so bleak. He was so skillful and committed to help me develop the same ability to reach my own capacity. So, why was I so unwilling to allow Randy to go for a fun spin on my motorcycle? Well, whereas Randy had a huge heart and so much to share about living to one's full capacity, there was one little problem—Randy had no arms.

Randy had lost his arms in an industrial accident. The sudden surge of electricity caused by someone throwing the power switch too soon killed his friend and left Randy, a young electrician, badly burned and barely alive. When he arrived at the hospital emergency room he was so near death that the surgeon on call had to physically threaten the anesthesiologist to do his job so that the surgeon could begin to operate.

There he sat on my large and powerful street bike with his powered prosthetic right arm and hand clutching the throttle (at 35 pounds per square inch) and his left hook trying to pull in the clutch. "This clutch is pretty smooth," he said with a big grin! "Now if I can just figure out how to get my prosthetic hand to twist the throttle, I'll be set!" He had pretty much convinced himself that it might just work. I, however, couldn't bear the experimentation. I had been with Randy too many times when his right arm would suddenly rise up because he got excited while talking and accidentally twitched the wrong muscle in his shoulder.

What is that inner quality some people possess that causes them to think that not having arms shouldn't stop them from riding a motorcycle, while others give up at the fist sight of a hang nail?

How is it that Joni Ericksen-Tada, paralyzed from the neck down, was able to become an award-winning painter by placing a paintbrush in her mouth? How do some people rise out of the ashes of a tragic childhood and become happy and productive friends, spouses, parents, and bosses while others are hopelessly enslaved to their tragedy? What is the difference between one couple growing and maturing, while another couple decides to call it quits from the same kind of conflict? How is one business leader able to endure the ups and downs of business and remain positive and respectful to those around him, while another becomes negative and abusive?

The greatest area of untapped potential in any organization is the personal capacity of its leaders.

If we as leaders could somehow apply the same dogged determination that Randy showed in learning to put on his own arms in the morning so that he could dress himself or figuring out how to pull change out of his pocket with his hook, we'd realize that we have capacity far beyond our current awareness. Leadership challenges and relational struggles give us a choice to look deep inside and mine the depths of all our inward capacity yet untapped or to blame-shift and give up. One clue for me is that Randy seemed to have resigned himself to the idea that he was going to look a little foolish at times; and that is okay. The biggest thing he lost was not his arms, rather it was the loss of his "ideal self" that caused the deepest grief and presented the greatest opportunity for growth.

Who of us, after all, would say that our life is proceeding according to script? Someone asked me just this week how I got into the leadership training business and I gave the truest and simplest answer I could: "I backed into it." That is how most people get into their ultimate career. We process the disappointment of the original plan and re-direct.

The paradox is that management of the inner game is the most difficult and yet it has the most impact on everything we do.

So many factors impact our inner game—how we feel about our key relationships, our finances, our career status, and our health—just to name some of the things that can pressure our inner world. The Bible says, "Above everything; guard your heart for out of it flow all the issues of life" (Proverbs 4:23). In working closely with hundreds of executives over the years I must attest that these words are so true.

The University of Illinois did a study on what makes leaders more effective and one of the factors they found that gave leaders a 40 percent increase in effectiveness was being involved in a church. The main reason was that leaders who were involved with a group of other learners on a weekly basis found themselves often in the environment where they were inclined to show up as a learner, admitting that they had not yet arrived. This helped them manage their inner game. So many times I've witnessed the walls of hostility or avoidance crumble when a key leader acknowledges his or her incompleteness and vows to continue to grow while leading.

Jim Collins, in his groundbreaking work in his two books, *Built to Last* and *Good To Great,* highlights a level five leader as one having a paradoxical blend of strength and humility. Leaders who freely acknowledge both their capacity and their brokenness solicit the loyalty and extra effort of those around them.

The truth is this, *we are all flawed and the difference between design and defect is how we display.* Some of my most treasured coffee mugs are wonderfully cracked and rugged looking. How silly and un-attractive it would be for me to try to cover up those imperfections with some extra clay. So too, it is ridiculous when we as leaders feel that we must attempt to cover up our flaws in order to be seen as po-werful, effective, and worthy of following. It's our flaws that give people a place to connect—to relate—not our smooth and glossy per-fection.

My second oldest, Sarah, was watching her grandmother put on moisturizing cream, as was her bedtime ritual, and asked, "Grandma, what is that cream for?"

To which Grandma replied, "Well, it's to take away the wrinkles."

Then Sarah (with the honesty of a first-grader) replied, "Well, it's not working!"

Ouch! The truth is that people who work for us and with us do not expect us to be flawless as leaders. They just want us to admit our flaws as we work to overcome them in their presence.

. . . to better understand limitations . . .

Life tells us, don't worry about limitations; just work harder, fast-er and longer. Unfortunately, however, that isn't always enough to get us past our greatest limitations. One of my clients called one day and asked me to meet with one of his top performers to see if I could figure out why he was experiencing such an uncharacteristic drop in his team's production. They had been the top producing team in the organization and the owner really depended upon the revenue from this group.

As the troubled employee and I sat eating dinner and chatting about life (not trying to push in too hard) he unwittingly offered up a clue to his suddenly sagging production. He told me a tragic story of losing his father whom he had been out of relationship with for two years since their business disbanded and left bad feelings between them. The breach was severe enough that not only had they not spo-ken in two years, but he didn't even go to his dad's funeral. The fami-ly was devastated and angry and he was stuck in unresolved grief.

The pressure of his grief over the loss and poor relational choices was pressing on him with an unrelenting heaviness and he was no longer able to navigate the typical pressures of managing a group of employees and responding to the needs of customers. The way I de-scribed it to him was that it was like he was driving around with the emergency break half on. It was not on enough to stop him—he was showing up every day and working hard—but it was on just enough to make it nearly impossible to achieve the same level of performance. All of the late nights and weekends couldn't overcome the true internal limitation that was holding him back.

When I began to prescribe an exercise for him to begin to address his unresolved and yet unprocessed grief, he buried his face in his hands and wept. Instantly he knew the path back to his old high performing work stature would lead him through honestly embracing the grief that had him emotionally handcuffed. Working longer hours and just trying harder wasn't going to cut it.

Our strongest limitations are often tangled up in the roots of deep fear and/or insecurity. The workplace doesn't leave much room for us to acknowledge such things, nor does our own need for ego stroke. We typically avoid anything that might cause us to look incompetent. So many times fights to the death in the boardroom driven by expressed anger could be avoided if one or both of the combatants would own the true emotional factors such as fear, abandonment, or sadness as the real emotional drivers of their behaviors.

One executive finally admitted to his boss that the origin of his non-responsive "deer in the headlight" behavior when his boss would rage at him had its roots in childhood trauma caused by a physically abusive step-dad. The raging behavior locked him up, but it just looked like passive aggressive defiance to the boss. Courage birthed honest disclosure, which led to deeper understanding and resolution. The entire leadership team benefited from the improved relationship of these two executives finally owning how their respective limitations hindered their professional relationship.

Our social context has great impact on our desire and ability to understand and openly embrace our limitations. So, the question is: what kind of work environment is most conducive to encourage honest self-awareness and courageous declaration of our struggles and limitations? How about insistence on growth not perfection, and authentic, risk-taking leadership from the top down? The way I like to say it is: Power Rests Upon Authenticity.

As leaders in an organization, we often struggle with the frustration that people just don't seem to want to own their failures and limitations. It is often not the mistakes that an individual makes that become the "deal killer," but their unwillingness to acknowledge them and seek help. Let me be clear: authenticity is not a "hall pass" on excellence. Quite the contrary, authentic leaders are more noticeably committed to excellence, attested by the fact that they are not willing to sacrifice quality and achievement for their own personal image management.

One day in talking with my client, he expressed his concern that one of his employees may not own his responsibility for a disappointing failure in their company under his watch. For this CEO, the inability of this supervisor to accept appropriate responsibility for an indiscretion of his direct report, would become a deal breaker and he really did not want to lose him. So I blurted out, "cup and bucket!" He of course looked surprised and was curious about what I meant. I asked him a question, "Is there any way (even if comparably very small) that you are responsible for any of the failure around this event?" He looked surprised, thought for a moment and said, "Yes, I suppose I am." Even though his responsibility in this failure was minor and secondary at most, I said to him, "If you want to ensure that this supervisor will take appropriate responsibility and extend his 'bucket of responsibility,' then extend your 'cup' first." This is called modeling and it is the surest way to transfer culture. We can not force people to show it when they blow it but we can model the behavior and show it when we blow it and in doing so, lead people to better understand their own limitations.

. . . commit to authentic change . . .

Authentic change can only happen when we first acknowledge the real problem! I watched a documentary on the building of the Titanic. One of the last-minute design changes they made was to create more seating capacity in the main ballroom so more people could sit for dinner. In the process, they reduced the amount of space for lifeboats. We all know the rest of the story. I've worked with sales people who have the most organized filing systems, the best looking brochures, and are great at writing proposals. They just have one little problem: they refuse to pick up the phone and make calls. That is what you call the "real problem" and the place where change needs to happen. They can buy all of the PDAs and cool binders they want, but until they address their fear of cold calling, authentic change won't happen.

The nice thing about identifying the real problem is that it is likely to lead us in the direction of finding *the right solution.* We can spin our wheels making adjustments that really don't address the main concern.

In a goal-setting session with a management team, one of the managers announced to his co-workers that he was going to spend more time creating more detailed reports. The reaction was immediate, loud, and in unison—"*No!*" The group went on to explain that that was the last thing he needed to do more of. They strongly encouraged him to spend less time at his desk and more time in the field working face-to-face with others. This is a great reminder that others can sometimes help us to more accurately target the right area of growth. Dare we ask?

I'll never forget the lecture I got from my tire guy after I expressed my frustration when a routine flat repair took much longer than it should have. "I had to completely rinse out the tire and then I had to go home and change my shoes and socks," he explained as I stood there rather annoyed and confused. "You used fix-a-flat didn't you?" he said with an accusing tone. "Yes," I said feeling like I had been caught! He went on to educate me that the way fix-a-flat works is to melt the rubber around the hole so that it covers over the hole. But if left in the tire it will ruin it. He even burned his toes when, while rinsing out the tire, it accidentally spilled out of the tire on his boot. What a powerful illustration about how the cure can sometimes be worse than the initial problem.

Authentic change usually takes a little longer, but the nice thing is, it will typically last longer as well. Life challenges us to skim the surface. Urgency can tempt us to use "fix-a-flat" instead of taking the time and committing the energy to "get our hands dirty" and "change the tire" on the spot.

A good way to gauge the direction we need to go to address the real problem and make authentic change is to notice what we are typically resistant to. At the risk of expressing a dim view, it seems to be one of the enduring principles of human nature that we often avoid the "heavy lifting" of making the core changes that can release the greatest amount of change and growth. Fear is a big factor. We are afraid that life won't wait for us to take the time or allow the "mess" to make the changes that will really make a difference. It is a rare work environment that endeavors to create the kind of climate that invites people into that space.

. . . and live in fuller realization of purpose, potential and destiny.

We are all searching for ultimate meaning and lasting impact in our lives. The problem is that it sometimes seems that the place we spend the majority of our waking hours (at work) is the hardest place to find it. No one wants on their tombstone: "Lived . . . Died . . . So

What!" We want our lives to matter. If we cannot find deep purpose, the challenge of our potential and whisper of our destiny in the place where we find the majority of our waking life, then everyone suffers. But let's face it—we are not all saving lives in the African outback or working on the cure to cancer. Some of our jobs seem ordinary and unimportant. It's all a matter of perspective.

One of my clients has a company that makes ball bearings for fighter jets. He was having a problem with keeping morale up and keeping the employees engaged in making sure they were meeting the meticulous manufacturing standards. He didn't think that they felt the full weight of how important their role was. So, he instituted a campaign designed to shift their thinking from making ball bearings for F-18s to making F-18s. He put a framed picture of an F-18 in every cubical. The campaign was successful. The greater purpose in their work had a direct impact upon production, turnover, profit, and overall employee satisfaction.

Often times, we will find that our greatest impact is not directly tied to the product we are producing, rather the people we are touching in the process. Whether they are internal or external customers, we have the opportunity to call them—yes, and maybe even lead them—into the kind of place that makes it safe for them to explore their deepest capacity, most frustrating limitations, and most exciting potential.

You see, Henry Ford was right when he said, "Why is it when all I want is a pair of hands, I end up getting the whole person?" Top organizations are committed to developing whole people. They recognize that in the end, superior products, happy families, and deep loyalty will be the result.

Dan McArthur

DAN MCARTHUR is the founder and president of InsideOut Impact, Inc. As a speaker, trainer, and life performance coach, Dan works with a variety of organizations helping them to deepen their leadership base, strengthen communication, and build high-performance teams. Dan has studied and spoken on the topic of outstanding leadership and has been actively involved in building dynamic teams for the past twenty years. Dan is known for approaching his topics with refreshing transparency and humor, and is committed to the idea that all behavior change and peak performance happens from the inside out. Dan has an incredible ability to challenge individuals and groups alike to take an honest look at the challenges they face and lead them to a place of inner motivation to take the next step in their journey to fully realize their potential. When Dan speaks, you will laugh out loud, you may cry a little, but for sure you will be surprised with how fast the time has passed.

Dan McArthur
10500 NE 22nd Place
Vancouver, WA 98686
Phone: 360.576.0470
E-mail: Dan@insideoutimpact.com
www.insideoutimpact.com

BEING THE LEADER IN YOUR OWN LIFE

BB Webb

How is your life going so far?

How do you *feel* about your life so far—your highs, lows, lessons learned, and your ability to regroup and move forward? Do you move forward with love, with passion, with aliveness?

Here's a dialogue I might have had with myself in the past if asked that question: "I'd never pretend my life has been easy, but then on the other hand, it's not been particularly hard. Well, yes, it has! (Pause.) How hard could it have been? I mean, I'm alive and well; I have a great business, wonderful friends, and I'm doing what I love. Compared to most of the world, well, of course my life hasn't been hard. How narrow and arrogant of me. (Pause.) Well, the '90s were a bitch—"

My point is that it all depends on who is looking and what our frame of reference is. No, compared with most people who are barely surviving in third world countries, and compare that with barely surviving in *our* country I'd say to myself, "Get a life, BB. Come on!"

The truth is, I have a life; it's unique, it's mine, and it can be looked at any way I choose. And so do you. And yes, my lows have been low and my highs have been high—as is the case for most of us. Though are we really being intentional about what we are creating in our lives? Certainly there is food on the table and we have lovely vacations, but what do you really want and who is leading your life? At the end of the day, were you proud of how you spent your time, your energy, your aliveness?

As spiritual beings having our rather unique human experiences, we are not different, although we are "individual." There is a difference. My thoughts are about being the authentic leader in my own life, step by step. Lack of heartfelt self-identification is a crisis of epic proportion.

How might you become a better leader in *your* own life? I propose we all start by leading ourselves and others through example. Having spent much time over the last decade studying energy healing, I am enthralled with the idea that as we heal ourselves, we heal others. When I think loving and good thoughts about other people, those thoughts not only raise *their* vibrations and level of wellness, but they raise *mine* as well. As I become more in touch with my own aliveness and passions, that energy vibrates and permeates everything I touch in a positive way.

Norman Vincent Peale was way more than right about the idea that "thoughts create things." They do far more than that—they create everything in our world.

Then versus Now

So, let's look at where we've come from and where we are now. Do you remember eighth grade? Think back! Didn't you want to pretty much be like everyone else, even though you thought you were really being unique? If it was the '80s for you, you had teased bangs that went up and out. For guys it was loose-fitting jackets with shoulder pads like Don Johnson of *Miami Vice.* If you were born in the '50s, as I was—the latter part of the Baby Boomer Generation—you either wore your hair with a part down the middle, and had combat boots on your feet (that was me—my mother thought I'd *never* wear heels!) or the latest in Villager or Lady Bug fashion, espadrilles—the works.

We want to be different but we want to fit in with everyone else. How many women reading this have at least thought about getting plastic surgery or Botox injections or have already gone that route? We want to look good, especially because our culture has told us what "good" looks like. Those bits of advice given to us on television, in magazines, and on the Internet keep our economy thriving! Whether it's thriving in a "good" direction or not is another question. I'm going to be fifty this year. I don't *feel* like what I thought fifty might be like and I *certainly* don't want to look like what I thought I would look like at fifty.

During the time my mother lived—from 1925 until her death in 1998—looking at life through "rose-colored glasses" was her perspective of choice. Further, her cultural choices were more limiting than had she lived today. Her children were all born in the fifties. On the other hand, during my era, for some of us, deep analysis and introspection have been the preferred modality from which to live, especially since we now have psychology gurus like Dr. Phil telling us how to behave and think, though sadly, with quite a theatrical spin to it all.

I think both perspectives have a purpose. One tries to look at the truth in the situation and the other maybe chooses not to engage because sometimes not engaging in certain dramas is a better choice. However, I don't mean to confuse this with what my mother more often than not employed—her "let's think happy thoughts" philosophy to keep peace at all costs. And the cost is great, especially when I'm really angry or certainly when I'm doing my best to grieve a loss, such as my divorce or, in fact, my mother's death.

What are you feeling?

Our feelings are meant to be felt and, using the grieving I had with my divorce as an example, it did not mean that staying married was what I wanted; but rather, the grieving was about the dream—the expectation I had had about a relationship that was no longer a reality. A mentor of mine reiterated that we must accept "things" for what they are before we can change them. So in my grieving I was able to mourn the loss of something I had expected to be "forever" in a certain way, which did not match the marriage I had.

In order to grow and evolve into the next chapter in my life I had to move through the hurt and come to the next place my soul was leading me to. It is with this very simple process that we become better leaders in our own lives—simple, although not easy in our current culture. We don't take the time to rest, eat, nurture ourselves, sit in quietude, or be with our loved ones, why in heaven's name would we take time to grieve or feel? It's much easier to numb that feeling through medication, overwork, food, or alcohol than to grieve! Oh, to wear my mother's rose-colored glasses, even though that comes at a terribly high price. We have a choice about how we move forward in our lives; we are in charge of our own growing consciousness concerning our world.

So, what are you choosing?

Your next growth question might be: "What *am* I doing?"

Who is making decisions for you? Why do you do what you do as a person, a woman/a man, a leader? How are you getting your information? From television, the Internet, on handheld computers, and e-mail?

My stepdaughter shared with me that the folks on *The View* thought the film *The Secret* was stupid. Based on that information she felt hesitant to watch the film. Before the advent of e-mail I had no idea there were so many options for having a larger penis. (Frankly, I really didn't and still don't care to know!) Information is coming in, whether we want it or not!

Your brainwashing came early and probably without ill intent. Your mom wanted this, your dad wanted that, your teachers led you this way, your church cajoled you that way, and the television—well, it's a really mixed bag.

A hundred years ago, an individual would meet, in person—face to face—on average about fifty people in his or her lifetime. That's about how many people individuals could compare and contrast themselves to. Even with the advent of television in the fifties, we'd see through the media and meet in person a limited number of people. Now, with more than nine hundred television stations available, the outpouring of films in our culture, the Internet, and of course travel, we "see" on average hundreds if not thousands of different people every day. We're not in Kansas anymore. (I'd better update my metaphor—does anyone still remember *The Wizard of Oz?*)

As you digest this overload of information, are you being true to who you really are or have you ever thought to ask the question? I believe we're moving into a time when it is *imperative,* not just circumspect, to ask the question, "Who am I and what do I really want?" It seems so simple.

Old systems are dying and new ones are being formed every moment and at lightning speed. Manifestations are happening almost instantaneously for those who believe they can. It is our job to become more conscious of why we do what we do and to acknowledge not just what we think, but first, what we feel in our hearts. And this is new to most of us.

As a very mind-centered, caffeinated, over-worked, over-drugged culture (prescription and non-prescription), tuning into what our bodies are telling us isn't typically where we go and it's not as easy to tune in as it maybe was at one time. There is just too much interference. We've long abandoned eating when we are hungry and sleeping when we are tired. Multi-tasking is unfortunately heralded as a heroic endeavor—we drive, talk on the phone, and drink our coffee, while the kids watch movies in the back seat. I had to remind my stepchildren to look up from their cell phones while text-messaging, when we were driving by the Empire State Building!

We've got drugs and delicious beverages to contradict our important body signals. And Starbucks stock continues to soar! Deadlines are set and ignored, tomorrow's work was due yesterday, our treadmill is moving at warp speed, and there are way too many expensive "things" we feel impassioned to work for to purchase. We've clearly lost touch with any messages from our body, our spirits, or a higher power who might want to whisper into our ear. It's no wonder that heart disease is the leading killer in our culture—our hearts have been sorely ignored.

Taking one step at a time, as "you can't get there from here"

I own and run a beautiful event venue in Georgia called Carl House where we host many corporate retreats and meetings as well as social events. Our main social events are weddings. I've taken a curious and circuitous trip around my world visiting a variety of careers during my life tour before becoming the owner of a special events venue. It's been an often tumultuous and fascinating journey and it continues to be so.

What I found most interesting and somehow alarming was that with each role I assumed, I had a *very* different sense of myself. Only with the advantage of time can I see how perfect each step was for bringing me to this grateful time and place in my life.

I began in my twenties fortunately not worried about my career path or marriage as many young women were. I thankfully got to work with a mentor who was a creative seeker. I discovered early on that so was I. I got to spend my twenties studying theatre, writing, traveling, exploring, performing, and finding out what made my passion come alive. There was then the issue of money at some point— eventually I had to figure out how to make a living. Although I toured and performed in a rather endearing one-woman play I'd written, I was not very good at creating more than a hand-to-mouth existence and frankly, I became very discouraged and exhausted. I landed in Atlanta and it felt like a fine place to live. On a hunch I stayed and today I still reside in the area, even though at the time I was at a loss as to what I'd do here.

Having swirled through a plethora of jobs, I was reminded of words of advice from a former theatre mentor, Tony Montanaro, an inspired "angel" in my life as a young woman. Wanting to bolt characteristically forward into a successful performing career, I frantically asked him, "Where do I go? New York? Should I tour? I really need to learn to move and dance better." This highly energized soul looked straight at me with his piercing eagle eyes and loving, open heart and responded, "Then why don't you go dance? Focus on learning to dance. Remember that you can't get there from here—you have to go step by step. Learn to dance and then take your next step." That was clearly not the answer I longed for from my beloved teacher. I wanted a clear map for taking me to a successful career as an actress. It wasn't until later that I understood the wisdom of his words. "You can't get there from here." He continues to reside in my heart as only a few special souls can.

Writing your own life—living from intention and with passion!

How aware are you of who you are, what feeds your soul, and what you need to feel *full* all by yourself? How open are you to exploring what really makes you thrive, feel alive, and want to get up in the morning? And how much responsibility do you take for making it happen yourself? How much of your personal power do you give away at every turn? Watch your attitudes and expressions and you'll be surprised. Where do you blame others, the traffic, the economy, your spouse, your parents, the weather, your weight, the "bug" that's going around?

Being co-creators of our own lives, we are each responsible for what we attract into it. With an attitude of curiosity as to what we are attracting, we can more quickly shift and bring in what fits our soul's purpose better.

Most of us are accustomed to looking for our wholeness outside of ourselves, although that never makes us whole. Listen to most of the popular songs on the radio! "You are my everything," "Without you I'll die," "Without you my life is not complete," and on and on. A heartfelt soul love is not only fulfilling, but it is also potentially part of *any* full life. Although losing your sense of wholeness when people come and go in your life is not healthy, grieving is different from losing who you are.

We attract what we already are. Take a look at who you have attracted into your life because they are direct reflections of you! What do you think of your landscape? Where do you give your power away to others? What do you do when you're in pain, depressed, sad?

My former pattern was to make frequent trips to the refrigerator, over-talk issues with extremely patient and tolerant friends, or watch non-stop movies about other people's messed up or "perfect" lives. You might shop or gripe about how "so and so did this or that" to you. Drinking is a nice diversion—my family of origin liked that strategy. I come by making parties happen naturally—my family is great at that!

Like cattle, many of us are just following the herd and have never posed such a question or even known that we could. We never dreamed we had a choice or if we did, we let the damaging voices of "can't, won't, shouldn't" drown out our "what ifs—our *possibility thinking*." But we can! The wonderful thing about change is it's *never* too late and it is our *only* constant in life.

I learned about "possibility thinking" while studying theatre and performing. To create a character in a play, you have to approach it with "what if" thinking. For example, *what if your character had been born in Peoria, Illinois, and your parents were divorced when you were seven, and your grandma helped raise you because your dad was not in the picture much. Your mother worked two jobs and wasn't around much either and your youngest brother had a disability that required special attention from all caregivers.* You begin to flesh out how that child might have grown up and what his or her worldview might have been as an adult. Based on what the playwright gave you, you had license to flesh out this character however you wanted beyond the words given. I'd love to play with how various characters could evolve based on background information and my imagination. How would they carry themselves, speak, behave around others, behave in private? The discovery would go on from there.

So what is the background of your "character"?

With that kind of analysis in mind, how did your history shape you and, more importantly, where do you want to go now? In my days as a performer I had a woman director who shared a book with me titled *Writing a Woman's Life*, by Carolyn G. Heilbrun. In her book, Heilbrun asserts that there are several ways a woman can write her life (or for that matter, I'd imagine a man as well). She can have a biographer write her life, she can write her autobiography or (and I love this), she can write her life a moment before she lives it. "Brilliant," I thought. And it is to this point that I also take exception.

How do you want to write your life and what supporting cast do you need to make it happen? All you need is a hunch on where you might want to go and the ability to listen for clues. Some patience helps, and stamina won't hurt, along with a healthy dose of *possibility thinking* or, to put it another way, the ability to risk a little to get a *lot!*

I've discovered over time that you don't need to have a detailed plan. In fact, that often inhibits the "bigger and better" plan that is waiting to show up in your life. However, like an athlete, you must have an intent and a focused mind and live not in your past or future, but in the moment where all possibility resides. More importantly, in order to be the leader in your own life, you must have an open and receiving heart and the ability to hear the quiet messages waiting to enrich your life.

Where I learned about "Faith" and the ability to "move forward as if"

As I alluded to earlier, a wise man has said to me not once but many times, "Nothing changes until it becomes what it is." That wise man is my therapist, Eddie Reece, who has graced my life with intriguing perspectives for many, many years now. He was quoting Fritz Pearls, the founder of Gestalt therapy. Fortunately, long gone are the days when being in therapy is viewed as a weakness. Now it is a way of looking into why we do what we do, raising our ability to reason and feel to a new level (at least with an excellent practitioner).

My real lesson in faith came not in a church, but in an Atlanta suburb, when I was forty-four, married just two years and for the first time. I had moved an hour outside of Atlanta to marry my now former husband and dear friend, Tommy. Frankly, I didn't feel I was giving up much by moving away from the city; I was floundering in Atlanta and had been looking for roots and a supportive partnership in my life. I moved to a not yet burgeoning area of the state, Barrow County. I knew no one and didn't have a job. Tom was infinitely supportive in giving me the freedom to discover what I wanted to do in this new life of mine. I ended up working with his company, but soon found that having two leaders in the same company—especially married leaders—did not work, at least not for us. And I wasn't passionate about his business.

I tried many things until one day, when handling the rental situation at the antebellum house he owned and had once lived in with his former wife, I happened to be listening to that little voice one sometimes hears in one's head (if not too distracted). I heard this voice suggest that this house could be a great place for people to gather and have parties. It was that simple. I was delighted that I'd actually *heard*—I'm not always a great listener and at that time was terrible at sitting quietly. I sat with that thought awhile and within twenty-four hours Tom grew excited as well. He had already experienced many of my "ah-ha" ideas for a business for myself, but something was different about this particular idea. I could feel it in my heart and in my gut.

We started with a small idea, taking some money we had saved, intending to do some minor fix-ups. As I interviewed other facility owners in the area and began to understand what the bridal and corporate business potential was, I grew more and more excited and clear about what we had to do to have a competitive advantage and how to best serve our clientele. Tom and I clearly switched our formidable roles, as he, with his strong business background, grew passionate about designing and restoring this gem of a house (which he did to perfection). On the other hand I couldn't sleep thinking about how I wanted to create, grow, and run this enterprise.

After much searching and hirings and firings to find the right mix of people to help us with our "little" project, with Tom's persistence we somehow were able to borrow almost two million dollars (and put an additional $80,000 on credit cards), and soon had business rolling in the door. Despite construction being delayed, endless rains throughout the spring, and set wedding ceremony dates that had to be rescheduled, with a determination to do what we knew was right to succeed with our dream (not cutting costs or sacrificing our growing vision), we learned about keeping the faith. In fact, we literally conjured it up, asking for help wherever it could be found and most importantly, "went forward as if"—as if we would succeed—and we did! Tom insisted that our entire endeavor "defied gravity," as we both felt it surely did.

Each of us has been forever changed and we are grateful for having had the opportunity to learn such a profound life lesson. Gravity can be defied, given the right attitude and intention!

Being the example: leadership as humanity

Our souls want to be known to us, and we must listen (this coming from a self-proclaimed "chatty" person). I continue to sit with the noise in my head, even though I am learning in small strokes to quietly hear my own inner wisdom so that I might direct myself intentionally and consciously forward. As I begin to merge my thoughts with my emotions, I create the life I am meant to live. As with the phenomenal popularity of the book, film, and CD of Rhonda Byrne's *The Secret,* we have the power to create, or rather co-create, our realities and to become leaders in our own lives.

I know too that I am given experiences to better know compassion for not just others, but for myself as well. I've learned to become curious as to what shows up in my life and where the gift is in its arrival. I've also learned to see the reflection of myself in others. My addictions are none other than places I've not yet fully developed or emotions I am unwilling to feel. To me it is all a part of my personal evolution and "becoming"—my continual "arriving." And, whatever I see and am tempted to judge in myself is clearly the place where I need to be in order to move into it or to shift somewhere else if I choose.

I encourage you to begin simply to notice your life, your choices, and your reactions. Be with your humanness without judgment, but with compassion and awareness. As you lovingly sit with what is, you will have the opportunity to change it and to begin to surrender to what feels real and authentic within yourself. Soon you will find yourself abandoning the struggle and embracing an unknown easiness. For, as it was with Dorothy in *The Wizard of Oz,* it's time for you to come home!

BB Webb

BB WEBB is the co-creator and owner of Carl House, an award-winning special events venue in Auburn, Georgia. She hosts radio and television programs in and around the Southeast. Trained in the performing arts, she toured the country with her original one-woman show until her 1993 arrival in Atlanta made her decide to grow roots there and become an entrepreneur. With interests ranging from authentic leadership to marketing to energy healing, style, elegance, and the perfection of "Twenty-first Century Southern Hospitality," the world is BB's stage and her audience adores the honesty, humor, reflections, and encouragement she gives them.

BB Webb, Owner
Author, Speaker, Radio and TV Host
Carl House, a gathering place
Phone: 770.586.0095
Fax: 770.867.7910
E-mail: bbwebb@carlhouse.com
www.carlhouse.com
www.carlcorporateretreat.com
www.bbwebb.tv

OPEN YOUR DESTINY

R. G. Williams

The key to success isn't in great talent! The key to success is to learn how to do something correctly, and then do it correctly every time! Do it the same way every time!

People look at great athletes, great artists, or great leaders and say, "They were born with that talent!" That is not true! We are all born with the abilities to learn and grow. What takes place throughout our lives is either constant encouragement or constant lack thereof. In other words, when our minds are encouraged and rewarded for a certain performance we strive to repeat that performance, which in return receives more encouragement and more reward. This is the upward spiral for abilities to flourish and become talents.

On the opposite end is the downward spiral. When a certain performance receives little or no encouragement or rewards, that performance usually is never repeated and therefore abilities become dull and eventually disappear altogether.

During the early informative years we must rely upon our parents, teachers, and peers to provide us with encouragement and reward. What is great about youth is that when one does not receive that stimulus from one area, we seek out an alternative place where we will receive positive reinforcements. However, should one never find positive feedback, over time he or she will stop searching for it and never develop inner abilities into talent!

As adults we have the capability to listen, learn, and process information. Then we have the power within to either store that information for future use or to discard it completely and only retain those things that will build us and not destroy us.

You and only you have that power. No one can take that power away from you unless you give it away. I continually hear the statement that someone has "hurt my feelings." *No one* can hurt *your* feelings unless you allow them to! They are your feelings and you are in control of you.

Maybe you are just hearing this concept for the first time or maybe you have heard it before, either way you must pay attention to your inner voice and develop the power within to control yourself and your emotions. Learn from everyone and every event you encounter. Process it, internalize it, or discard it and move forward.

One way to strengthen your abilities and maintain your focus is to focus on the "where" of your life instead of the "why." The where of your life is a matter of sitting down and taking the time to discover who you truly are. This can be a simple and quick process or it may take some deep soul-searching in order to find out what truly makes you tick. Many times you will discover that certain habits you continually perform do not have anything to do with who you are! When this happens you should rejoice because you have the power to change! You have the power to make the decision as to who you are going to be from this point forward and no longer will you allow a non-beneficial habit to control you.

Once you discover who you are, then it is time to design who you want to become and where you want to go. This becomes the "where" in your life. Once you get to know your inner self, design who you want to be and where you want to be in life, you will gain tremendous power over the daily obstacles. Challenges will jump out at you every day, however, once you truly understand yourself and have the "where" defined, those obstacles lose their power over you, and you will walk forward with unwavering inner confidence. The "where" creates the spiritual strength that works from within, gives you the internal drive, and prepares you emotionally for everything that crosses your path. Having a heart-to-heart conversation with yourself, defining who you are, who you want to be, and where you want to be not only internalizes everything, it now gives you the power to control yourself.

From the outside people will notice a difference. You will begin to hear statements such as, "What have you done—you look different [or happy]," etc. Remember that external appearances are driven from internal manifestations! What you feel on the inside will appear on the outside in one form or another, it is inevitable! You cannot always maintain a "poker face." So as you fine-tune your internal programming, your external appearance will improve and will become contagious. Have you ever encountered someone you did not know and then after the encounter you're left with a feeling that you wanted to get to know that person better? This feeling was most likely caused by the other person's internal confidence and peace. On the other hand, you may have encountered someone you couldn't wait to get away from! That feeling is caused by the other person's internal turmoil manifesting itself on the outside.

Life is a series of moments. Each and every one prepares you for the next moment. You will encounter great moments as well as not so great moments and it will be up to you to understand how every moment works into your future.

One decision that I made during my heart-to-heart with myself was to look at every moment as a learning process—what can I learn from this? Positive or not, it does not matter; each moment or event brings with it an opportunity for you to learn, process, internalize, or discard. So many people look at things and focus on what went wrong. I suggest that you look at everything and ask yourself "what can I learn from this?" You will find that your focus will become clearer and your activities will have purpose instead of simply walking through life haphazardly. We have all heard the question: "Is the glass half empty or half full?" I say that if you see the glass as half empty, you need to get a smaller glass! Always look at the positive and how it benefits you in your quest for your "where."

As you embark on anything new—a new career, a new task around the house, a new relationship, etc.—you are going to meet with obstacles and even brick walls. This is the time when you will be glad that you took the time to have the heart-to-heart talk with yourself, defined who you are and who you want to be, and designed the "where" in your life.

The "where" pushes you beyond anything you could ever imagine. It is like climbing to the top of a mountain and when you reach the top you look around and think, "Wow, look at all of the other opportunities that are out there for me!" Focusing on the "where" in your life allows you the confidence to focus on what you are becoming, not on what you are.

Once you have designed what you want and where you want to end up, it is time to reverse engineer your plan. Reverse engineering is starting at the end result and moving backward, identifying each step along the way until you arrive at where you currently stand. Reverse engineering your plan or your life is the purest form of Stephen Covey's statement: "Begin with the end in mind."

One of the simplest ways to accomplish this is to look at your plan differently and more importantly, look at how you write your plan differently. Writing down your plan of action is the key to inner peace when turmoil enters your pathway. You will encounter situations daily that will test your plan and will push hard against your inner spirit. Having a clear understanding of who you are and where you are going will give you the power to stay focused on your plan as well as give you strength to protect your inner spirit. Once you have taken the steps to discover yourself and design the "where" in your life, your action plan should become very clear.

You may have previously taken time to sit down and write out your goals and maybe even a plan of action only to then let that paper collect dust along with all of the other action plans or "New Year's resolutions." You get caught up in the day-to-day hum-drum routines and lose sight of the plan. Then another year goes by and you find yourself in the same place you were, only now you are a year further down the path.

Your plan of attack is critical to your growth both internally and externally. A plan of attack helps you clarify your priorities. Why is that so important? When things that are important to you and your priorities are not in alignment, then you will be sending conflicting and confusing signals to your subconscious or "super-conscious" mind. When you send a conflicting message your brain will default to previous habits that are not necessarily in line with your new game plan. In other words, you will continue to perform the old habits, thus creating more frustration and confusion, which adds to the downward spiral—the complete opposite of what you want! Conflicting signals cause confusion, and a confused mind is never productive! On the other hand, when you are crystal clear on your priorities and your plan of attack, you will send clear and concise signals to your super-conscious mind that will then allow you to achieve the desires of your heart! A plan of attack is more than just words on paper—it is the guide-rails for your race track called life!

What is the difference between a plan of attack and goals? Goals should be viewed as guideposts along the way to your end result. You can even use them as rewards along the way. A plan of attack is when you have discovered your "where" and reverse engineered back to where you were at any given moment in your life.

I read a story from Thomas Watson, founder of IBM, that illustrates reverse engineering at its best. When he was asked what he attributed the phenomenal success of IBM to, he is said to have responded: "IBM is what it is today for three special reasons. The first reason is that, at the very beginning, I had a very clear picture of what the company would look like when it was finally done. You might say I had a model in my mind of what it would look like when the dream—my vision—was in place.

"The second reason was that once I had that picture, I then asked myself how a company that looked like that would have to act. I then created a picture of how IBM would act when it was finally done.

"The third reason IBM has been so successful was that once I had a picture of how IBM would look when the dream was in place and how such a company would have to act, I then realized that unless we began to act that way from the very beginning, we would never get there. In other words, I realized that for IBM to become a great company it would have to act like a great company long before it ever became one.

"From the outset, IBM was fashioned after the template of my vision. Each and every day we attempted to model the company after that template. At the end of each day we asked ourselves how well we did, discovered the disparity between where we were and where we had committed to be, and at the start of the following day set out to make up for the difference. Every day at IBM was a day devoted to business development, not doing business. We didn't do business at IBM, we built one!"

Discovering your inner self and inner strength, designing your "where," reverse engineering, and a plan of attack will give you the power to stop simply "living" and help you create a "life."

The next step in rising to the top is to "act as if you have already reached your goals." This is like the assumptive close. When you are making a sales call you should always approach it as if you already have the sale in hand—*this sale is going to happen*—act as if your success is for certain. "Act as if" you have already accomplished the task or the opportunity. "Act as if" simply means you are progressing with silent confidence or the assurance that what you have already put into play has been accomplished. Everything you thought about during your heart-to-heart discovery and everything that you have designed with your "where" has already been successful. Once you commit and "act as if," the energies and everything that surrounds you begins pushing you forward toward the ultimate goal.

Without acting as if everything has been accomplished or that your future is secured, you allow negative energies, fears, reluctance, guilt, and hesitancy to control your life.

When you play at half speed in sports, the business world, and more importantly, in life, you are going to get hurt! My dad always said, "Some people work fast and others work half-fast!" Too many people play this game of life "not to lose" instead of "playing to win!" Why would you want to always go through life holding back? Why not design everything you want and then open the throttle and go to work building your life?

As I have consulted with people over the years, I have heard a common theme from the Baby Boomer Generation. That common theme was, as they were reaching retirement, they began to realize that their lives had not turned out the way they had hoped or envisioned. In fact, many of them made comments such as, "What if I had done this or that?" "If only I had taken advantage of . . ." "I am too old now, but when I was younger . . ." What they began to realize was they had planned out their life through *forward engineering* and many of them had not planned anything!

Let's look at the current system that has been created for us to follow:

During the early years we are so focused on play time—"Who can I go play ball or dolls with?" "What am I going to do after school?" We watched movies or television and read books and developed heroes—people we wanted to become like when we grew up. We acted out being a fireman or policeman or businesswoman, etc. As the years continue and we progressed through school, we began to solidify or abandon those heroes for new heroes or people we wanted to become.

Then we became seniors in high school and reality started to hit us. We were then faced with difficult choices to make—do we get a job or do we go onto a university? We wondered, will a scholarship help me with schooling or am I faced with working a full-time job and part-time school? We had the feeling we could conquer anything, which is the way it should be. Some were so confident they did not take the time to develop a plan as to how they were going to succeed!

During the senior year of high school, everyone is exposed to the possibilities of continuing education at different universities. Nationwide school systems provide a "career day" for seniors where university and military recruiters set up booths in the gym to share with the graduating class what their organizations have to offer. With this exposure, as well as outside exposure, the majority of the graduating class begins to map out, through *forward engineering*, what they are going to do for the rest of their lives!

I believe the first mistake made is that we are taught to plan our lives without knowing where we want to end up. *Forward engineering* is starting wherever you are and planning each step ahead of you as you go. *Reverse engineering* is looking out at the future and designing what you want, then working backward to where you currently stand.

The major difference between these two processes is that once you implement *reverse engineering* you can keep your eye on the prize as you move forward without having to worry about each step ahead of you. Think about how many start out at a university with a chosen major, only to change their major after a couple of years of late night cramming for tests. The reason people change their major after spending a couple of years of their lives headed in one direction is because they begin to redesign their "where."

So much time and energy would be better utilized by starting out designing where you want to be and who you want to be in the end. This way, the choices made would be in harmony with your inner self, sending clear and concise signals to your brain.

Once you have your plan in place, then it is time to go to work. You must learn what consistent action and constant work truly means. Consistent action means that you have your plan and are implementing each step of that plan. Constant action means that you are doing the same thing over and over again. The repetition of simple things leads to an inevitable explosion. It means that you remain true to your plan.

It is said that "practice makes perfect." I disagree. A better statement would be *"perfect* practice makes perfect." You could show up to a driving range to hit a bucket of golf balls and while practicing, your form could be completely incorrect. You could hit bucket after bucket and spend hundreds of hours on the golf course, but because your form is incorrect you will never play golf like the greats unless you learn correct form. Learning what must be done to correctly hold the golf club, swing correctly, and reading the course will move you light years ahead of the competition.

In life, in doing the same habit over and over again without fine tuning or "perfect practice," you will have nothing more than the same habit. You then find yourself confused as to why you are where you didn't want to be and wondering why you aren't where you thought you would be.

While working your plan you must manage your energy. Life is a marathon, not a sprint. You will find certain windows of opportunity when you have to use bursts of energy. Much like a track and field meet, certain events require bursts of speed to move a runner into a stronger position. Your life will require different levels of energy or commitments from you to accomplish your plan. By designing your life and knowing your "where," you will be prepared at all times and know when and where to increase performance within yourself. Consistently working and constantly staying on task helps manage your energy and keeps you focused for the entire plan. Working your plan of action toward your "where" will give you power over what is going on in your life at any given moment. It will also give you the inner confidence to handle everything that is thrown your way.

When writing goals, most people focus on monetary goals only. I will be the first to admit that having money is comforting, knowing that the bills are paid with some extra left over. However, money, by itself, is not a motivator. Money is simply an outside measurement of accomplishments. Money is neutral and doesn't care who owns it. It reflects a mirror image of who you are on the inside. What you do with money reveals everything. Money makes good people great and bad people worse. If your goals and what you focus the use of money on is not in harmony with your plan of where you are or who you are becoming, you will forever be in conflict with yourself. Understanding where you are in your plan and how focused you are on your plan will give you power over the control of money. Money becomes a by-product or an added bonus as you work toward your end result. In other words, money doesn't define you—the car you drive, the clothes you wear, your watch collection, a pen with a star on it, where you dine, the circles you walk in, the magazines or newspapers you read, etc. do not define you! The challenge is that almost everything tells us that all of those things should be what defines us.

When you truly focus on being where you want to be and how you want to develop your lifestyle, money naturally comes. It is similar to a dog chasing its tail—as soon as the dog realizes that all he has to do is go forward and his tail will follow, he can stop running in circles. So many people run in circles chasing an unknown without ever getting anywhere and then find out that once they get what they are looking for, they don't know what to do with it. The sad fact is that when they do in fact get it, it is too often not what they wanted anyway.

By focusing on money instead of your "where," you will find yourself unfulfilled and confused as to why you feel that way. This is much like driving down the freeway not knowing which exit to take and then wondering how you got to where you are!

You must treat money as numbers and not your lifestyle. Most people never take the time to define what money is and what money means to them. We are not taught the importance of understanding money. We go through school being taught how to make money, yet we are never taught what to do with the money when we earn it. We are not taught saving principles or how to spend wisely, so we never really have a concept about what money is.

The other area most people neglect is that they never take the time to define their life and therefore their focus becomes driven by material things only. Lifestyle covers every area of your life. When you look at all areas of your life powered by a deep understanding of the "where" in your life, you will empower yourself to accomplish your dreams and goals. When you turn your focus on your internal passion, the money will follow and you will become satisfied internally as well as externally. Allowing money to control the "where" and "when" of your lifestyle will lead you down a very lonely path and will always leave you wanting more of something, but you will never be able to put your finger on what that something is.

When writing down your plan of action, you must understand the difference between *wealth* and *riches*. Too many people confuse these terms; they talk about being wealthy when in reality they are talking about being rich. Wealth comes in the form of healthy children, the ability to get out of bed and put your feet on the ground every day, friendships, quiet time with someone special, etc. These things are true wealth. Riches come in the form of dollars and because these two terms are not clearly defined, it opens the door to confusion and chaos internally. *Remember*, a confused mind is never productive.

I believe that I am the wealthiest person on the planet and that is what gives me the inner confidence and strength to move forward in all areas of my life. Riches will be added as I choose to take advantage of opportunities. Clearly defining wealth and riches will allow you to see that opportunities are plentiful. Your inner self will begin to see these opportunities instead of your external eyes deceiving you.

The last two areas that you must address in your lifestyle plan of action and your "where" that will allow you to rise to the top are:

1. *"Give credit where credit it due."*
2. *"Pay it forward."*

I have always lived by the statement that you "check your ego at the door" or you "put it in your pocket." You are who you are because of the multiple influences in your life. No one is self-made because something like that can never be accomplished on your own—you must have outside influence. Whether you are selling products or services, somebody had to buy or consume what you were selling. There is always someone involved in the process.

I believe that humility is your standing before God—who you are internally. Poverty is a state of mind! You must give credit where credit is due because then you are keeping your ego in check. The challenge you will face when your ego gets in the way is it will blow out the candle of your mind and you will once again be in a state of chaos and confusion. Allowing the energy to flow back to those who participated in your plan of action and your success will allow the energies to get behind you and help push you forward faster.

I truly believe that a selfish person is one who seeks everything without purpose and this blocks the flow of energy. Your plan of action will no doubt have you pursuing knowledge, relationships, wealth, and riches. Yet I believe that it is selfish for you to allow that pursuit to stop with you and not flow through you. In other words, where much is given, much is expected. When you receive and then sit back and hold on to all that you have learned, you are blocking the flow. It is critical for you to understand that once something is learned then it is your responsibility to share it with others and allow the energy to flow freely.

Receiving wealth and riches and then not allowing them to flow through you is very detrimental to your internal growth. Paying it forward is simply *"what goes around comes around—plus!"*

Take the time to focus on the "where" in your life, reverse engineer your plan, and then work constantly and consistently with your eyes focused on your mark and you will find internal joy and satisfaction. This in return will manifest externally and you will find yourself "rising to the top!"

R.G. Williams

R.G. WILLIAMS is an active real estate investor, educational trainer, and one-on-one motivational mentor.

R.G. has been successfully investing in real estate for over ten years. Currently he invests nationally as well as internationally with properties ranging from single- and multi-family residences, to commercial properties and developments.

R.G. is a published author in Real Estate with training manuals, and monthly articles in Real Estate magazines. He is a featured guest speaker to Investors Associations nationwide as well as Real Estate agencies and brokerages. He is a frequent guest on *Real Estate Round Table* and other syndicated television and radio shows. He was nominated to the "Who's Who of Professionals."

R.G.'s mentoring specialties include but are not limited to: Real Estate, Business Consulting and Development, Personal Development, Financial Management, and Debt Freedom. He has been instrumental in the development of the coaching and training curriculum for Creative Learning Institute, Real Estate Investor Support, RESuccessgroup, and Dr. A. D. Kessler.

R.G. is adept at helping others achieve higher levels of success and dreams in their lives by helping them see things from a different perspective and keeping them accountable to those dreams and goals.

R.G. is the CEO of "Creative Real Estate Academy of Training—CREATE," a member of the Board of Directors for "Invest in Kids" and co-Founder of the "Rosas Humanitarian Foundation," an organization that is building a hospital for the town of Lo Arado, Mexico.

R.G. Williams
Open Your Destiny
4535 W Sahara Ave., Ste. 200
Las Vegas, NV 89102-3622
Phone: 801.403.0053
www.openyourdestiny.com

FINDING YOUR PASSION

Troy Rackley

I grew up playing football my entire childhood life. It was my passion. I loved the competition and being with my friends. We lived in the projects on the North side of Akron, Ohio, and we were very poor. Sports were all we had and two of my siblings had a sport that they excelled at. My sister, Ginger, was an amazing track star and my brother, Garfield, was the best overall athlete in football and basketball. Robert is my oldest brother; his focus and accomplishments were in academics.

My junior year in high school was a tough year for my family because my mother was raising four children by herself and working to help put my brother, Robert, through college. I remember my mother being tired all the time from working two to three jobs. She did this to ensure that we always ate well and my brother was able to become one of the first people in the projects to go to college and earn his degree.

I was scheduled to graduate in two years and I wanted to make sure we were in a better situation financially so that my mom wouldn't have to work so hard. It was apparent that my skills on the football field were improving with age and my coach told me that I was good enough to play in the National Football League. I was very moved by this because NFL or not, I loved playing the game of football. It was at that point when I understood the process of getting into college via playing football. My coach told me that if I received a full scholarship my mom wouldn't have to pay one red cent for my college education. I was very relieved by the thought of not having my mom go through all that exhaustion to ensure I had a bright future.

I made a commitment to myself that I would use my talents on the football field to achieve a full scholarship and make my mom proud and not put a strain on the family financially. My sister and my other brother went to vocational school and they paid their own way. I wanted to be an engineer so I knew I needed to go to college.

I dedicated my senior year to my mom and set out on my quest to demonstrate that I had skills worthy of receiving a full scholarship to play football at the college level. I was in the best shape of my life and I was determined that nothing was going to stop me from achieving that goal.

It was the night before the first game of my senior season and I went to the opposing team's bonfire to "talk some trash." The team was burning a replica of my jersey. This meant that I was considered a threat to their chance of winning the game.

On game day I was pumped as never before and I prayed that I would have a great season. On the very first play of my senior season we kicked off and I made the tackle; but during the pile-up, one of the opposing team members twisted my ankle and broke it. I didn't realize this until later so I limped off the field thinking I had sprained it. I asked the trainer to re-tape it for me. I played the rest of the entire game and we won.

After the game I removed the tape from my ankle, which was starting to swell like a balloon. I was taken to the hospital for x-rays. The x-ray revealed my worst nightmare—there were bone chips that showed my ankle was indeed broken. The doctor said that I would be out for eight weeks and we only had nine weeks left in the season. I thought my dream of getting a full scholarship was shattered.

I told the doctor that it was unacceptable for me to stay out for eight weeks. I asked him why I couldn't play with a rubber cast like the professionals do and he said that the hospital didn't do that type of thing. Fortunately for me I was well known in the city. A local Kent State University coach was in the hospital at the time and told me that if I would come and visit their school as a part of the official visits he would provide me with a rubber cast so that I could play football for the rest of the season. I immediately agreed to visit with the stipulation that the visit was no guarantee that I would sign with them.

My dream was starting to come back. It was decided that I would not practice in full contact for the rest of the season and just play in the games. I was originally a right defensive end so to protect my left ankle my position was changed to left defensive end.

When it came to game two it was noticed by the opposing team that I had an oversized ankle and a bit of a limp. On the first play on defense the opposing team's running back came to block me and he went right for my ankle with his helmet. I was able to block his helmet from hitting my ankle with my right hand. After the play I realized that I had hurt my hand and went to the sideline to have it taped. The coach told me I couldn't play with my hand that way because it looked like I had broken it. He taped it anyway at my request. I played the rest of the game and went to the hospital afterward.

I had my hand x-rayed and sure enough, it was broken. I picked up the phone and called my contact at Kent State University and asked him if he could make a rubber cast for my hand. The coach complied. I played the rest of the season with a broken left ankle and a broken right hand. My position then switched to roving linebacker so I could protect my limbs.

At the end of the season I had a number of schools talking to me and it became clear that I was going to get a full scholarship to play football.

My mom was very proud of me for my achievement until she understood that had I played with two broken limbs to achieve it. My dream had come true because I was passionate about what I was doing and I loved it.

When I started my career as a supervisor it became obvious to me that the experience I had gained from sports was going to be a key asset when it came to working in a team environment. I really enjoyed helping people achieve their goals. As my career grew and I had more responsibility, it became apparent to my superiors that I had an interpersonal style that allowed me to reach people on a level that was very motivating and insightful. It was noticed by all of my managers that I had a coaching style that allowed me to get the most out of every team that I managed.

I really looked forward to coaching my people and helping them, so when I realized that my goal was to help others achieve theirs, I thought I would take this natural skill I possessed and become a coach.

I have been told that my passion is contagious. When people love what they do, they have energy and excitement when they talk about what they do. That is true in my life. I found my passion and I absolutely love what I do. When people gave me feedback, saying that I had changed their life, I knew that this was my life's calling. My grandmother once told me that God put me on this earth to serve and help others and ever since that moment my passion—coaching—was born. Coaching is not what I do, it's who I am.

Have you ever watched Michael Jordan compete in basketball? Have you ever watched Tiger Woods compete in golf? These are two of the world's most well-known athletes and they play their game with a lot of passion. Both Michael and Tiger demonstrate a love for their jobs. It's funny to think that their sport is their job, but it is what they get paid to do. Michael and Tiger found their passion in their sports. They are considered a benchmark for everyone to find their passion in their career.

My question to you is why can't all people love what they do to that extent? In the corporate world there are a lot of people who work in jobs that they really don't like and they are very unhappy.

What is your answer to the following questions: Do you love what you do from a career standpoint? Are you passionate about it? Does what you are doing drive you toward your goals? Do your goals have anything to do with your current job?

If you have answered no to any of the above questions, *why do you continue to work there?* I have worked in corporate America for nineteen years and I know what it is like to wake up in the morning and go to a job that I didn't really like. When we are not passionate about what we do, our energy becomes drained, and our minds become closed and stagnant. We start accepting the status quo of mediocrity.

Take some time to answer the following questions:

- If I could create my own job, what would I be doing?
- How productive would I be at work if I were passionate about what I'm doing?
- If I loved what I do at work, how would that influence other parts of my life?
- Do I believe in myself?
- What is stopping me from finding my passion?

We will take question one first: if I could create my own job, what would I be doing?

As we know from what I said about Michael Jordan and Tiger Woods, it is possible to love what you do. We know professionally what excites us such as a certain type of project, working on a particular team, or creating the ideal work environment. What type of work could you do that would be challenging, stimulating, and fun? If you can answer these questions you can be on your way to finding your passion. What basketball and golf is to Michael and Tiger, your job can be the same to you if you allow yourself to be passionate about what you do at work.

Think about the type of work you would be doing if you had the same passion toward your job as Michael and Tiger. When was the last time you had so much fun at work that it didn't seem like work? When was the last time where the hours went by so fast during the day that you didn't even notice that it was time to go home? You can create such a role but it is no surprise that you may need to change your environment or workplace in order to achieve such greatness.

Michael and Tiger found their passion early in life but it wasn't until they took it up to another level that the world recognized their greatness. All we want in corporate America is for our managers to see our greatness because after all, after college, corporate America is our version of where most professionals "play" just like the NBA or PGA.

Question two: how productive would I be at work if I were passionate about what I'm doing?

I believe we have all had the experience at work where there are people, projects, or even specific tasks that energize us. When you are passionate about your work you will excel at it and look to create more value naturally. Most people do things that they have to do on projects or specific job tasks that meet the minimum expectation. However, if you had the opportunity to take ownership of something and your employer acknowledged that and rewarded you for it, your productivity would continue to increase. As the saying goes, "If you love what you do, then it's not work."

Michael and Tiger love their jobs and they are very productive because of it. Why can't we be the same way? We can! When separating life into three thirds we can see the importance of being productive. Take the twenty-four hours that are in a day: some people work eight hours a day, some people need eight hours of sleep a night, and the other eight we have for family and other activities.

I don't know anyone in the corporate world who has such a balance but the first third—work—really consumes most of our daily life. When things get off balance at work we start dipping into our other two thirds. We start sleeping less, spending less time with the family, and being unhappy overall. If you really enjoyed what you do you would not cheat as much on the other thirds. You spend a third of your weekly work-life at some type of job so it is very important that you enjoy what you do because life gets shorter when you cheat the other thirds.

Question three: if I loved what I do at work, how would that influence other parts of my life?

Has anyone in your circle of friends or family ever said you should leave your job? Has anyone ever said that you work too much and don't have time for anything else? Has anyone ever said, "Don't take it out on me because you had a bad day"? We are all going to have bad days but just as in sports, if you have a tough day and lose the game, the season is not over. We have to re-group and understand what we need to do in order to get back on track.

I have met a number of people who have told me that when they leave the office, all the stress and worry is left at the door before they get home. Well, I don't believe it's that simple. If you know people who love what they do, look at their energy levels, work-life balance, and overall general health. If you have a family, how would a healthy work-life impact home life? We have all put in the long weeks and we seldom have time or energy to do the things we love to do on weekends because for many of us the work-week tends to shift. If we had the time to balance, there would be other things we could find to do. We would continue to make the excuse that we just can't fit everything in that week.

When you have a frustrating exchange at work, do you talk about it at home? Do you bring the frustration home? I'm not saying that just because you love what you do, you will never have a bad day or skip exercise; but the odds are that if you are happy at work, the rest of your life outside of work could be more productive. The bottom line is: are you living the life you want? Are you in the career you want? Are you taking what life gives you as opposed to creating the ideal opportunity that will make you feel in total control of your own destiny?

Question four: do I believe in myself?

Self-confidence is a worldwide problem and involves a lot of people. Sometimes we have to have the right support system in place to assist us in being more confident. If your environment (people around you at work or even at home) is toxic, then it is hard to have the confidence to chase your dreams and find your passion. You must first find out what you like and then seek some feedback from those you are close to and trust to see if they see the qualities in you that you see in yourself in the same area.

Believing in yourself is very difficult if you are starting from low self-esteem; but in order to be on the road to finding your passion, you must start there. Some people have a fear of failure and for that reason they doubt themselves. When people ask me, "What if I fail?" I say, "What if you don't?" Most of the responses I have heard are disbelief—some people just don't think success is within them.

I learned another poem by Edgar A. Guest that sums it up when it comes to giving up on yourself. The very fitting title of this poem is *See it Through:*

When you're up against a trouble,
Meet it squarely, face to face;
Lift your chin and set your shoulders,
Plant your feet and take a brace.
When it's vain to try and dodge it,
Do the best that you can do;
You may fail, but you may conquer,
See it through!

Black may be the clouds around you
And your future may seem grim,
But don't let your nerve desert you;
Keep yourself in fighting trim.
If the worst is bound to happen,
'Spite of all that you can do,
Running from it will not save you,
See it through!

Even hope may seem but futile,
When with troubles you're beset,
But remember you are facing
Just what other men have met.
You may fail, but fall still fighting;
Don't give up, whate'er you do;
Eyes front, head high to the finish,
See it through!

I would challenge you to memorize this poem so that when you start to doubt that person in the mirror, you say to yourself SIT (See It Through).

Question five: what is stopping me from finding my passion?

When I joined my fraternity (Omega Psi Phi) I had to memorize a poem and it goes like this:

Excuses are the tools of incompetence
Used to build monuments of nothingness;
Those who use them are seldom good for anything else.

Excuses are like comfort food. We feel better and we have justified even in our own minds that we feel better about why we are not achieving our desired goals.

This had a profound impact on me because we tend to make excuses all the time when we don't reach our goals. When it comes to exercise how many times do we say, "I just don't have time"?

I grew up in a single-parent household and my mother ("Super Woman") worked two jobs, kept food on the table, paid her car payment, and never missed any of my football games.

We never have time for the things that matter most to us and we use every excuse we can think of to make ourselves comfortable with our answers.

One of the main things stopping a lot of people from finding their passion is not knowing what it is. Sometimes we get into such a routine of mediocrity and complacency that we just give up and take what life gives us. We have to take our lives and control our own destiny. The number one thing that is stopping you from finding your passion is *you.*

One excuse that people use when asked the question, "What is stopping you?" is the fact that most people have not only forgotten what really makes them happy, but also how to get to their goals. I say that you have to have a plan.

In football and basketball, every coach puts together a game plan to win. Think about it: every single play is designed to score. If all players execute their jobs, then they should score every single time. However, sometimes the skills on the opposing team are superior and one team or the other falls short of their goal (to score). How many times have you seen a team walk off the field in defeat because they didn't score every time?

Just as in sports, our plan will not be without areas that need improvement. First and foremost we must have a backup plan when a strategy doesn't work. We have to be determined to succeed with our plan for personal greatness. When it comes to our goals we have to be selfish for a change. When we can learn to do that, we focus on the core of who we are and we begin to re-define ourselves to the point of re-inventing ourselves. We must have an attitude that we don't believe in permanent barriers—we know that every play won't work but we will not quit the game. We will develop a game plan that has contingencies in the event we have roadblocks.

There is no reason I can think of why we should not have the same passion for our jobs that some of the super stars I mentioned earlier have for their jobs. Early in life they developed a talent for their sport and worked really hard to excel at it. One thing to consider is that not everyone makes it to the big time like Michael and Tiger.

If we continue with the athlete analogy, we realize that there are people who just love the game they play. You see little kids who find their passion in sports when they sleep with a basketball or football. That child likes feeling what we all felt when we were doing something that we really loved doing when we were kids. We can re-create this feeling as adults in our work life. The only thing that has changed is the rules of the game to compete. For some jobs we now have to have a certain level of education, specific experience, or professional qualifications. If we have those things it is now time to get the child-like enjoyment back.

When we make excuses about why we can't achieve our personal/professional goals, we deny ourselves our rightful happiness. Do you deserve to be happy with what you do from a work standpoint? This answer is an obvious yes for 99.9 percent of people.

Every day when we wake up to go to work we will have challenges that may set us back just like the football play that didn't score. We must condition ourselves just the way athletes do to play in the game of work. Finding your passion can be tough because the working world is full of politics, roadblocks, and people who will challenge you in ways that may be disruptive to your road to success.

One of the challenges to finding your passion might include being resilient when it comes to the politics, roadblocks, and people. What you have to remember is that poem, *See it Through.* We have to keep our eye on the prize of finding our passion and not let anyone determine our outcome of success on our behalf. When you work in an environment like that you have to remember, one of the biggest keys to being resilient is the fact that whatever the situation is, *you choose your response to all situations.*

When you hit a roadblock that someone has deliberately put in front of you, your response might be, "That person really frustrated me by doing that." My response is that you chose to feel frustrated. If you really think about it, other people my trigger an emotional response in us but it is our responsibility to choose how we react. We have to condition our mind to grasp the concept that finding our passion is not just our goal, it's our destiny. When you get there, you will know that you have arrived when you say, "I love my job."

Have you ever noticed how people who perform their jobs with passion seem to have the innate ability to inspire others? If you have ever participated in any form of game in your life such as competitive sports, you will notice that true competitors will say that the better competition, the better they play. People who are inspired will lift their game to the next level of performance. In this case the people who have that ability to inspire others do so just by having passion for their skills in the role that they are performing.

The closest example to this happened in my own household. My wife, Christine, had been working in cardiac rehab her entire career. Just like most people who perform the same job over and over, she found herself in a rut. She has always enjoyed helping people and in her case it was helping people recover from a heart attack or stroke. She was constantly learning new ways of reaching people who really wanted to change their behaviors post trauma. In her role in cardiac rehab she was splitting her time between rehab and the fitness center. In the fitness center, just like most fitness experts, she was helping people who wanted to change their habits and become healthier before they would have to see her in cardiac rehab. Part of her job was illness recovery and the other part of her job was illness prevention.

She was so inspired by the prevention part of her job that the company offered her a role on the prevention side of the fitness center. She was asked to attend classes to receive her wellness coaching certification. She came home one day and told me, "I have found my passion and it is consistent with yours. I want to help people with wellness on the prevention side of health risk factors." I had never seen her glow like that. She decided that she was going to put her efforts into becoming a licensed wellness coach. She found her passion through helping others achieve their wellness vision and goals.

For most people, to find their passion they must first define their dream job. When you sit back and think about that dream job, you realize that you can love what you do and the first facial expression that comes to mind is a smile when you think about it for the first time. That smile could be quickly turned upside down when you think of your starting point and all that you have to accomplish to reach that goal if you are in a situation where you don't enjoy what you do. Finding your passion might be the easiest thing to do; but the difficult decision you have to make is do you follow your dreams and try and achieve it, or is life just too hard?

Life is too short to not follow our dreams because if we only leave one legacy in this world it should be that we lived life to the fullest and the type of work we did was very rewarding and fulfilling.

The first step in this process is to understand your own level of self-awareness. Contrary to popular belief, you don't have to be an expert in what you do initially, but it does require hard work.

When Michael Jordan entered the NBA he was just another professional basketball player who loved the game and what the game did for his life; but he worked very hard to become the best in his era.

When you are passionate about what you do, you are a constant learner and if you have the leadership skills, you are also a constant teacher. In the book, *Good to Great,* Jim Collins wrote about the "hedgehog concept." The premise of the hedgehog concept was that the companies that went from good to great interconnected three concepts:

1. What are we deeply passionate about?
2. What drives our economic engine?
3. What can we be the best in the world at doing?

If you really think about it, individuals who have found their passion can go from good to great by following this very same concept. It is not just a coincidence that companies subscribe to the concept of being passionate about what they do. When you really sit back and think about companies, you quickly realize that they are made up of individual people. Imagine a company that has defined its hedgehog concept (the three points above) and a team of individual people who have found their passion and working in such an environment. All that together would have the makings of one of the greatest companies to work for in the world. The work environment alone would be enough to encourage people to do their best work.

I believe the type of senior leadership that will keep companies growing will be those who have the ability to tap the innate talent in their people. Employees would be placed in roles they are passionate about and watch themselves excel and help others grow. That organization will thrive with success.

One sure way to get to the top in your own life (notwithstanding the corporate ladder) is love what you do and work with people who love what they do. I guarantee that the atmosphere will be electric and the people around you will notice a change in you. They will be very envious of that and will want it in their life.

I found my passion and I was fortunate enough to help inspire my wife to find hers. I can tell you from current experience that when you love what you do it makes for a happy household. Whether you are already at the top or on your way, find your passion and help others to find theirs. I can confidently assure you that you will never work another day in your life because just like Michael, Tiger, my wife, and me, you will be just having fun. Fun has always been better than work, but you can reach the point of not knowing the difference between the two when you find your passion. I am living proof.

Troy Rackley

TROY RACKLEY unlocks the door of his clients' potential and then watches as they walk through it. He helps people see the possible from the impossible. Troy Rackley provides these insights as both a motivational speaker and as an executive coach. Troy gained his drive early by using his athletic ability and learning from his mother's struggles as a single parent to escape from the projects of Akron. He achieved a successful twenty-year career as an executive with Fortune 50 companies within the United States and Australia. His unique ability as an engineer, coupled with his understanding of human capital, gives his clients a unique perspective as they partner with him in developing their success. If you have career aspirations for upward mobility and are looking for passion, then take the stroll to your door with Troy, open it, and begin to see the impossible as possible.

Troy Rackley
The Next Level of Performance, LLC
P.O. Box 622393
Oviedo, FL 32762-2393
Phone: 407.803.3487
E-mail: Troy@coachthenextlevel.com
www.coachthenextlevel.com

ಆ ಕ ಬಂ

A Special Interview

Jack Canfield

David E. Wright (Wright)

Today we are talking with Jack Canfield. You probably know him as the founder and co-creator of the *New York Times* number one best-selling *Chicken Soup for the Soul* book series. As of 2006 there are sixty-five titles and eighty million copies in print in over thirty-seven languages.

Jack's background includes a BA from Harvard, a master's from the University of Massachusetts, and an Honorary Doctorate from the University of Santa Monica. He has been a high school and university teacher, a workshop facilitator, a psychotherapist, and a leading authority in the area of self-esteem and personal development.

Thank you for being with us today.

Jack Canfield (Canfield)

Thank you, David. It's great to be with you.

Wright

I talked with Mark Victor Hansen a few days ago. He gave you full credit for coming up with the idea of the *Chicken Soup* series. Obviously it's made you an internationally known personality. Other than recognition, has the series changed you personally and if so, how?

Canfield

I would say that it has and I think in a couple of ways. Number one, I read stories all day long of people who've overcome what would feel like insurmountable obstacles. For example, we just did a book *Chicken Soup for the Unsinkable Soul.* There's a story in there about a single mother with three daughters. She contracted a disease and she had to have both of her hands and both of her feet amputated. She got prosthetic devices and was able to learn how to use them. She could cook, drive the car, brush her daughters' hair, get a job, etc. I read that and I thought, "God, what would I ever have to complain and whine and moan about?"

At one level it's just given me a great sense of gratitude and appreciation for everything I have and it has made me less irritable about the little things.

I think the other thing that's happened for me personally is my sphere of influence has changed. By that I mean I was asked, for example, a couple of years ago to be the keynote speaker to the Women's Congressional Caucus. The Caucus is a group that includes all women in America who are members of Congress and who are state senators, governors, and lieutenant governors. I asked what they wanted me to talk about—what topic.

"Whatever you think we need to know to be better legislators," was the reply.

I thought, "Wow, they want me to tell them about what laws they should be making and what would make a better culture." Well, that wouldn't have happened if our books hadn't come out and I hadn't become famous. I think I get to play with people at a higher level and have more influence in the world. That's important to me because my life purpose is inspiring and empowering people to live their highest vision so the world works for everybody. I get to do that on a much bigger level than when I was just a high school teacher back in Chicago.

Wright

I think one of the powerful components of that book series is that you can read a positive story in just a few minutes and come back and revisit it. I know my daughter has three of the books and she just reads them interchangeably. Sometimes I go in her bedroom and she'll be crying and reading one of them. Other times she'll be laughing, so they really are "chicken soup for the soul," aren't they?

Canfield

They really are. In fact we have four books in the *Teenage Soul* series now and a new one coming out at the end of this year. I have a son who's eleven and he has a twelve-year-old friend who's a girl. We have a new book called *Chicken Soup for the Teenage Soul and the Tough Stuff.* It's all about dealing with parents' divorces, teachers who don't understand you, boyfriends who drink and drive, and other issues pertinent to that age group. I asked my son's friend, "Why do you like this book?" (It's our most popular book among teens right now.) She said, "You know, whenever I'm feeling down I read it and it makes me cry and I feel better. Some of the stories make me laugh and some of the stories make me feel more responsible for my life. But basically I just feel like I'm not alone."

One of the people I work with recently said that the books are like a support group between the covers of a book—you can read about other peoples' experiences and realize you're not the only one going through something.

Wright

Jack, with our *Speaking of Success* series we're trying to encourage people in our audience to be better, to live better, and be more fulfilled by reading about the experiences of our writers. Is there anyone or anything in your life that has made a difference for you and helped you to become a better person?

Canfield

Yes and we could do ten books just on that. I'm influenced by people all the time. If I were to go way back I'd have to say one of the key influences in my life was Jesse Jackson when he was still a minister in Chicago. I was teaching in an all black high school there and I went to Jesse Jackson's church with a friend one time. What happened for me was that I saw somebody with a vision. (This was before Martin Luther King was killed and Jesse was of the lieutenants in his organization.) I just saw people trying to make the world work better for a certain segment of the population. I was inspired by that kind of visionary belief that it's possible to make change.

Later on, John F. Kennedy was a hero of mine. I was very much inspired by him.

Another is a therapist by the name of Robert Resnick. He was my therapist for two years. He taught me a little formula called E + R = O that stands for Events + Response = Outcome. He said, "If you don't like your outcomes quit blaming the events and start changing your responses." One of his favorite phrases was, "If the grass on the other side of the fence looks greener, start watering your own lawn more."

I think he helped me get off any kind of self-pity I might have had because I had parents who were alcoholics. It would have been very easy to blame them for problems I might have had. They weren't very successful or rich; I was surrounded by people who were and I felt like, "God, what if I'd had parents like they had? I could have been a lot better." He just got me off that whole notion and made me realize the hand you were dealt is the hand you've got to play and take responsibility for who you are and quit complaining and blaming others and get on with your life. That was a turning point for me.

I'd say the last person who really affected me big time was a guy named W. Clement Stone who was a self-made multi-millionaire in Chicago. He taught me that success is not a four-letter word—it's nothing to be ashamed of—and you ought to go for it. He said, "The best thing you can do for the poor is not be one of them." Be a model for what it is to live a successful life. So I learned from him the principles of success and that's what I've been teaching now for more than thirty years.

Wright

He was an entrepreneur in the insurance industry, wasn't he?

Canfield

He was. He had combined insurance. When I worked for him he was worth 600 million dollars and that was before the dot.com millionaires came along in Silicon Valley. He just knew more about success. He was a good friend of Napoleon Hill (author of *Think and Grow Rich)* and he was a fabulous mentor. I really learned a lot from him.

Wright

I miss some of the men I listened to when I was a young salesman coming up and he was one of them. Napoleon Hill was another one as was Dr. Peale. All of their writings made me who I am today. I'm glad I had that opportunity.

Canfield

One speaker whose name you probably will remember, Charlie "Tremendous" Jones, says, "Who we are is a result of the books we read and the people we hang out with." I think that's so true and that's why I tell people, "If you want to have high self-esteem, hang out with people who have high self-esteem. If you want to be more spiritual, hang out with spiritual people." We're always telling our children, "Don't hang out with those kids." The reason we don't want them to is because we know how influential people are with each other. I think we need to give ourselves the same advice. Who are we hanging out with? We can hang out with them in books, cassette tapes, CDs, radio shows, and in person.

Wright

One of my favorites was a fellow named Bill Gove from Florida. I talked with him about three or four years ago. He's retired now. His mind is still as quick as it ever was. I thought he was one of the greatest speakers I had ever heard.

What do you think makes up a great mentor? In other words, are there characteristics that mentors seem to have in common?

Canfield

I think there are two obvious ones. I think mentors have to have the time to do it and the willingness to do it. I also think they need to be people who are doing something you want to do. W. Clement Stone used to tell me, "If you want to be rich, hang out with rich people. Watch what they do, eat what they eat, dress the way they dress. Try it on." He wasn't suggesting that you give up your authentic self, but he was pointing out that rich people probably have habits that you don't have and you should study them.

I always ask salespeople in an organization, "Who are the top two or three in your organization?" I tell them to start taking them out to lunch and dinner and for a drink and finding out what they do. Ask them, "What's your secret?" Nine times out of ten they'll be willing to tell you.

This goes back to what we said earlier about asking. I'll go into corporations and I'll say, "Who are the top ten people?" They'll all tell me and I'll say, "Did you ever ask them what they do different than you?"

"No," they'll reply.

"Why not?"

"Well, they might not want to tell me."

"How do you know? Did you ever ask them? All they can do is say no. You'll be no worse off than you are now."

So I think with mentors you just look at people who seem to be living the life you want to live and achieving the results you want to achieve.

What we say in our book is when that you approach a mentor they're probably busy and successful and so they haven't got a lot of time. Just ask, "Can I talk to you for ten minutes every month?" If I know it's only going to be ten minutes I'll probably say yes. The neat thing is if I like you I'll always give you more than ten minutes, but that ten minutes gets you in the door.

Wright

In the future are there any more Jack Canfield books authored singularly?

Canfield

One of my books includes the formula I mentioned earlier: E + R = O. I just felt I wanted to get that out there because every time I give a speech and I talk about that the whole room gets so quiet that you could hear a pin drop—I can tell people are really getting value. Then I'm going to do a series of books on the principles of success. I've got about 150 of them that I've identified over the years. I have a book down the road I want to do that's called *No More Put-Downs,* which is a book probably aimed mostly at parents, teacher and managers. There's a culture we have now of put-down humor. Whether it's *Married With Children* or *All in the Family,* there's that characteristic of macho put-down humor. There's research now showing how bad it is for kids' self-esteem when the coaches do it so I want to get that message out there as well.

Wright

It's really not that funny, is it?

Canfield

No, we'll laugh it off because we don't want to look like we're a wimp but underneath we're hurt. The research now shows that you're better off breaking a child's bones than you are breaking their spirit. A bone will heal much more quickly than their emotional spirit will.

Wright

I remember recently reading a survey where people listed the top five people who had influenced them. I've tried it on a couple of groups at church and in other places. In my case, and in the survey, approximately three out of the top five are always teachers. I wonder if that's going to be the same in the next decade.

Canfield

I think that's probably because as children we're at our most formative years. We actually spend more time with our teachers than we do with our parents. Research shows that the average parent only interacts verbally with each of their children only about eight and a half minutes a day. Yet at school they're interacting with their teachers for anywhere from six to eight hours depending on how long the school day is, including coaches, chorus directors, etc.

I think that in almost everybody's life there's been that one teacher who loved him or her as a human being—an individual—not just one of the many students the teacher was supposed to fill full of History and English. That teacher believed in you and inspired you.

Les Brown is one of the great motivational speakers in the world. If it hadn't been for one teacher who said, "I think you can do more than be in a special ed. class. I think you're the one," he'd probably still be cutting grass in the median strip of the highways in Florida instead of being a $35,000-a-talk speaker.

Wright

I had a conversation one time with Les. He told me about this wonderful teacher who discovered Les was dyslexic. Everybody else called him dumb and this one lady just took him under her wing and had him tested. His entire life changed because of her interest in him.

Canfield

I'm on the board of advisors of the Dyslexic Awareness Resource Center here in Santa Barbara. The reason is because I taught high school with a lot of kids who were called at-risk—kids who would end up in gangs and so forth. What we found over and over was that about 78 percent of all the kids in the juvenile detention centers in Chicago were kids who had learning disabilities—primarily dyslexia—but there were others as well. They were never diagnosed and they weren't doing well in school so they'd drop out. As soon as a student drops out of school he or she becomes subject to the influence of gangs and other kinds of criminal and drug linked activities. If these kids had been diagnosed earlier we'd get rid of a large amount of the juvenile crime in America because there are a lot of really good programs that can teach dyslexics to read and excel in school.

Wright

My wife is a teacher and she brings home stories that are heartbreaking about parents not being as concerned with their children as they used to be, or at least not as helpful as they used to be. Did you find that to be a problem when you were teaching?

Canfield

It depends on what kind of district you're in. If it's a poor district the parents could be on drugs, alcoholics, and basically just not available. If you're in a really high rent district the parents not available because they're both working, coming home tired, they're jet-setters, or they're working late at the office because they're workaholics. Sometimes it just legitimately takes two paychecks to pay the rent anymore.

I find that the majority of parents care but often they don't know what to do. They don't know how to discipline their children. They don't know how to help them with their homework. They can't pass on skills that they never acquired themselves. Unfortunately, the trend tends to be like a chain letter. The people with the least amount of skills tend to have the most number of children. The other thing is that you get crack babies (infants born addicted to crack cocaine because of the mother's addiction). In Los Angeles one out of every ten babies born is a crack baby.

Wright

That's unbelievable.

Canfield

Yes and another statistic is that by the time 50 percent of the kids are twelve years old they have started experimenting with alcohol. I see a lot of that in the Bible belt. The problem is not the big city, urban designer drugs but alcoholism. Another thing you get, unfortunately, is a lot of let's call it familial violence—kids getting beat up, parents who drink and then explode—child abuse and sexual abuse. You see a lot of that.

Wright

Most people are fascinated by these television shows about being a survivor. What has been the greatest comeback that you have made from adversity in your career or in your life?

Canfield

You know it's funny, I don't think I've had a lot of major failures and setbacks where I had to start over. My life's been on an intentional curve. But I do have a lot of challenges. Mark and I are always setting goals that challenge us. We always say, "The purpose of setting a really big goal is not so that you can achieve it so much, but it's who you become in the process of achieving it." A friend of mine, Jim Rohn, says, "You want to set goals big enough so that in the process of achieving them you become someone worth being."

I think that to be a millionaire is nice but so what? People make the money and then they lose it. People get the big houses and then they burn down, or Silicon Valley goes belly up and all of a sudden they don't have a big house anymore. But who you became in the process of learning how to do that can never be taken away from you. So what we do is constantly put big challenges in front of us.

We have a book called *Chicken Soup for the Teacher's Soul*. (You'll have to make sure to get a copy for your wife.) I was a teacher and a teacher trainer for years. But because of the success of the *Chicken Soup* books I haven't been in the education world that much. I've got to go out and relearn how do I market to that world? I met with a Superintendent of Schools. I met with a guy named Jason Dorsey who's one of the number one consultants in the world in that area. I found out who has the best selling book in that area. I sat down with his wife for a day and talked about her marketing approaches.

I believe that if you face any kind of adversity, whether losing your job, your spouse dies, you get divorced, you're in an accident like Christopher Reeves and become paralyzed, or whatever, you simply do what you have to do. You find out who's already handled the problem and how did they've handled it. Then you get the support you need to get through it by their example. Whether it's a counselor in your church or you go on a retreat or you read the Bible, you do something that gives you the support you need to get to the other end.

You also have to know what the end is that you want to have. Do you want to be remarried? Do you just want to have a job and be a single mom? What is it? If you reach out and ask for support I think you'll get help. People really like to help other people. They're not always available because sometimes they're going through problems also; but there's always someone with a helping hand.

Often I think we let our pride get in the way. We let our stubbornness get in the way. We let our belief in how the world should be interfere and get in our way instead of dealing with how the world is. When we get that out of that way then we can start doing that which we need to do to get where we need to go.

Wright

If you could have a platform and tell our audience something you feel that would help or encourage them, what would you say?

Canfield

I'd say number one is to believe in yourself, believe in your dreams, and trust your feelings. I think too many people are trained wrong when they're little kids. For example, when kids are mad at their daddy they're told, "You're not mad at your Daddy."

They say, "Gee, I thought I was."

Or the kid says, "That's going to hurt," and the doctor says, "No it's not." Then they give you the shot and it hurts. They say, "See that didn't hurt, did it?" When that happened to you as a kid, you started to not trust yourself.

You may have asked your mom, "Are you upset?" and she says, "No," but she really was. So you stop learning to trust your perception.

I tell this story over and over. There are hundreds of people I've met who've come from upper class families where they make big incomes and the dad's a doctor. The kid wants to be a mechanic and work in an auto shop because that's what he loves. The family says, "That's beneath us. You can't do that." So the kid ends up being an anesthesiologist killing three people because he's not paying attention. What he really wants to do is tinker with cars. I tell people you've got to trust your own feelings, your own motivations, what turns you on, what you want to do, what makes you feel good, and quit worrying about what other people say, think, and want for you. Decide what you want for yourself and then do what you need to do to go about getting it. It takes work.

I read a book a week minimum and at the end of the year I've read fifty-two books. We're talking about professional books—books on self-help, finances, psychology, parenting, and so forth. At the end of ten years I've read 520 books. That puts me in the top 1 percent of people knowing important information in this country. But most people are spending their time watching television.

When I went to work for W. Clement Stone, he told me, "I want you to cut out one hour a day of television."

"Okay," I said, "what do I do with it?"

"Read," he said.

He told me what kind of books to read. He said, "At the end of a year you'll have spent 365 hours reading. Divide that by a forty-hour work week and that's nine and a half weeks of education every year."

I thought, "Wow, that's two months." It was like going back to summer school.

As a result of his advice I have close to 8,000 books in my library. The reason I'm involved in this book project instead of someone else is that people like me, Jim Rohn, Les Brown, and you read a lot. We listen to tapes and we go to seminars. That's why we're the people with the information.

I always say that your raise becomes effective when you do. You'll become more effective as you gain more skills, more insight, and more knowledge.

Wright

Jack, I have watched your career for over a decade and your accomplishments are just outstanding. But your humanitarian efforts are really what impress me. I think that you're doing great things not only in California, but all over the country.

Canfield

It's true. In addition to all of the work we do, we pick one to three charities and we've given away over six million dollars in the last eight years, along with our publisher who matches every penny we give away. We've planted over a million trees in Yosemite National Park. We've bought hundreds of thousands of cataract operations in third world countries. We've contributed to the Red Cross, the Humane Society, and on it goes. It feels like a real blessing to be able to make that kind of a contribution to the world.

Wright

Today we have been talking with Jack Canfield, founder and co-creator of the *Chicken Soup for the Soul* book series. As of 2006, there are sixty-five titles and eighty million copies in print in over thirty-seven languages.

Canfield

The most recent book is *The Success Principles*. In it I share sixty-four principles that other people and I have utilized to achieve great levels of success.

In 2002 we published *Chicken Soup for the Soul of America.* It includes stories that grew out of 9/11 and is a real healing book for our nation. I would encourage readers to get a copy and share it with their families.

Wright

I will stand in line to get one of those. Thank you so much being with us.

Jack Canfield

JACK CANFIELD is one of America's leading experts on developing self-esteem and peak performance. A dynamic and entertaining speaker, as well as a highly sought-after trainer, he has a wonderful ability to inform and inspire audiences toward developing their own human potential and personal effectiveness.

Jack Canfield is most well-known for the *Chicken Soup for the Soul* series, which he co-authored with Mark Victor Hansen, and for his audio programs about building high self-esteem. Jack is the founder of Self-Esteem Seminars, located in Santa Barbara, California, which trains entrepreneurs, educators, corporate leaders, and employees how to accelerate the achievement of their personal and professional goals. Jack is also the founder of The Foundation for Self Esteem, located in Culver City, California, which provides self-esteem resources and training to social workers, welfare recipients, and human resource professionals.

Jack graduated from Harvard in 1966, received his ME degree at the university of Massachusetts in 1973, and earned an Honorary Doctorate from the University of Santa Monica. He has been a high school and university teacher, a workshop facilitator, a psychotherapist, and a leading authority in the area of self-esteem and personal development.

As a result of his work with prisoners, welfare recipients, and inner-city youth, Jack was appointed by the state legislature to the California Task Force to Promote Self-Esteem and Personal and Social Responsibility. He also served on the board of trustees of the National Council for Self-Esteem.

Jack Canfield
Worldwide Headquarters
The Jack Canfield Companies
P.O. Box 30880
Santa Barbara, CA 93130
Phone: 805.563.2935
Fax: 805.563.2945
www.jackcanfield.com

ACT LIKE AN ENTERPRISING CEO TO RISE TO THE TOP

Vickie L. Milazzo, RN, MSN, JD

To reach the top, personally and professionally, you must act like the people who are already at the top. Top CEOs like Oprah Winfrey and Donald Trump, no matter how different their approach, have one key quality in common: they are enterprising. Enterprising CEOs manage life from the driver's seat. They choose their destination, make their own road rules, and cash the big checks.

Reward doesn't have to appear as dollars in the bank, but an enterprising CEO does expect a payoff. What ultimate reward will you receive from rising to the top? A new Porsche? An Italian villa? An exotic vacation to Poughkeepsie? A promotion? Or simply to make a difference in the world? Getting in touch with that payoff—knowing the "why" in the "want"—tells you whether your enterprise is a true goal or passing fancy. Knowing "why" sustains your commitment to follow through, rise to the top, and reap the payoff you desire.

When you think about it, life is the grandest enterprise of all—and you're in charge. Top CEOs know they are not only CEOs of their companies, but enterprising CEOs of their lives. You manage your personal development, finances, public relations, transportation, commissary, entertainment, janitorial services, and even human resources. You're already the CEO of the business of running your life, fully vested in the payoff, so why not act the part and take on your next exhilarating enterprise?

I bellied up to this concept in 1982 when I decided it was time to act like the CEO of my life and career instead of an employee. I discovered the enterprising secrets of top CEOs, left my hospital job as a registered nurse earning $28,000 per year, and launched what is today a $16 million business.

The same twelve CEO secrets of enterprise I used to launch my business and grow it annually for twenty-six years will help you rise to the top as CEO of your life and career.

CEO Secret 1: Everything Is Marketing

The old saying among entrepreneurs, that nothing happens in business until "somebody sells something," is equally true in life. From the moment you were old enough to realize that a smile could "sell" your parents on giving you another cookie, you've been marketing your ideas.

Getting a promotion or pay raise means selling your supervisor on your abilities, attitude, and experience. That's marketing.

Convincing your spouse it's okay to leave the dishes or television and cuddle up for some intimacy may require charm and persuasion. That's marketing.

Convincing your property owners' association to resurface the tennis courts might require a benefit analysis and presentation. That's marketing.

Corralling a widely separated extended family for a reunion will mean selling the idea, date, and place to all family members. That's marketing.

You may not work in the marketing department, but getting a promotion, lining up a new date, or changing an associate's thinking means selling your ideas.

When I received my master's degree in nursing, I learned the hard way that this valuable asset had no value unless I marketed it. No one at the hospital said, "Thank you for pursuing higher education, Vickie. Here's the pay raise you deserve." So I attempted to market that idea to my manager. She didn't buy in, so I marched my asset out the door to market elsewhere. My new employer received the benefit of my expanded knowledge, and I got the pay raise I deserved.

The best idea goes nowhere without strong, innovative marketing behind it.

Marketing has three simple parts: First, find a need. Second, fill that need. Third, convince people to buy in. As CEO of your life, start viewing everything you do from this three-part marketing perspective.

What need will you fill? A promotion-seeking customer service rep (CSR) with a flair for marketing spots an opportunity to demonstrate her expertise for growing the company and making the manager's life easier. A mother invents a game to occupy her children and recognizes a niche in the toy market for such a game. A multicultural high school teacher sees a need for training business travelers in the social graces expected at their foreign destinations.

How will you fill that need? To move to a marketing position, the CSR must impress the marketing manager with his or her ideas while continuing to fulfill the responsibilities of a current position. The mother must perfect her game along with a plan for production and distribution. The teacher must develop a training package and sell it to the business world.

Who, specifically, will buy into your idea? While the CSR's company pays the salary for his or her promotion, the marketing manager must buy in first. A toy company will probably have to buy into a mom's idea before parents do. The teacher must sell his or her multicultural experiences to corporate training departments before employees sign up.

Envision your bold enterprise. Before investing any significant resources into your idea, describe your venture and answer the question, "What will this do for me?" Write down in detail the payoff you desire—a job, a stunning piece of jewelry, a relationship, a promotion, or simply happiness. Bestow your vision with sensory detail. See, hear, taste, and feel it. The more real it is to you, the more you'll believe in your ability to make it happen.

Communicate your enterprising idea with energy and confidence. You have a story to tell and you have to make it interesting, believable, and credible. Is your story intriguing? Does it show how your idea will solve a real problem? Does it include the practical aspects? Does it highlight your knowledge and skill?

Be authentic. Your message must not only be interesting but also real. "Own" your message. Draw the core of your presentation around the concept of filling a need. Demonstrate how your ideas, products, or participation will benefit the person or company you're marketing to, then prove why you're the right match for your idea. In the end, it has to hold together. The CSR has to shine and deliver. The entrepreneur mom has to produce a game kids will tell their friends about.

The teacher has to send business travelers abroad adequately prepared.

Connect with your audience. Companies we call "super brands" make customers feel special just for buying the product and smart for owning it. Make sure you connect in a way that allows people a glimpse into your world. Reinforce your message in everything you do. More than "service with a smile," give "service with feeling." Make customers want to seek you out to work with you again.

Repeat your story often. Not everyone will get it, not everyone will buy in. But every aspect of your life is a marketing opportunity. Keep polishing your presentation and spreading the word.

CEO Secret 2: Be Your Own Number One Fan

CEOs promote their company and their achievements. They know that buyers don't want to purchase from losers. Announcing your achievements may feel boastful, but can you imagine Oprah or "the Donald" being shy about broadcasting their triumphs?

With humility, let people know any time you score, whether it's finishing a big project, winning an award, expanding your services, or being asked to speak at the company banquet. Who you know is important, but even more important is who knows you. Achievements are your resume and they expand your credibility. Announcing your achievements also validates the choices people have made on your behalf—the boss who promoted you or the buyer who purchased from you wants to know that he or she has bet on a winner.

Write a note. Send newsworthy communications to your friends, family, coworkers, and acquaintances. Be concise, stir in a little humor, and people will look forward to receiving your news. When my book *Inside Every Woman* made the *Wall Street Journal* bestseller list, I not only sent out news releases but I also informed friends, family, and professional colleagues through a variety of e-mail messages.

Roll out a news flash. Craft a short, punchy message and tack it onto your voice mail message or place a hyperlinked tagline under your e-mail signature. Everybody likes to know a winner.

Get a friend to post your news on listservs and blogs. This can be done as a well-crafted question addressing the interests of a specific forum. You'll get valuable third-party credibility and possibly start some buzz about you and your enterprise.

CEO Secret 3: Expect Icebergs

No enterprise is unsinkable; the Titanic sank its first time out. Plenty of entrepreneurs have made and lost millions on their rise to the top. But in acting like a CEO, you'll create such a solid foundation and framework for your enterprise that only an enormous iceberg can knock you off course.

Happily, not all icebergs are bad. Sometimes a minor catastrophe forces you to steer in a new direction that changes your business for the better.

In 1990 I hit an iceberg when my largest clients dissolved their firm. The source of dependable income I'd grown to count on vanished. Fortunately, I had the necessary lifeboats in place. My business stayed afloat, and the changes I made took me on an adventurous and profitable detour. If I had missed the iceberg, I might also have missed an opportunity for major advancement. Losing those significant clients gave me time to focus on my passionate vision— education and speaking—a path I wouldn't otherwise have taken. (Of course, the iceberg could have sunk me instead.)

Assess your strengths and challenges. The stability of your enterprise comes not only from how you handle day-to-day routines, but more importantly, from how you engage your strengths when an iceberg pops up unexpectedly. Challenges may involve expertise, competition, or getting along with your supervisor. By knowing what you have in reserve and frequently reassessing the waters ahead of you, you can maneuver with confidence.

Be honest. Research reveals that men typically overrate their abilities while women typically underrate theirs. A fair, honest assessment will help you develop the necessary strengths or marshal the outside resources you'll need.

Be willing to risk hitting icebergs. You have to sail before you can fail. You can maneuver around icebergs, but if you never leave the dock, you'll never have an enterprise to keep afloat. If you're not out there in a big way, you won't risk but you also won't win.

Often it's not hitting the iceberg but fear of hitting it that drowns you. How many people resist changing jobs or leaving a bad marriage only to realize afterward that it was the best decision they ever made? Jane Austen, the famous English novelist, chose not to marry out of her poor background but to pursue her dream of writing—in a time when women writers were considered "scandalous." She braved the iceberg. Soon she'd written six of history's most important works of English literature. If she'd married any of her suitors, she may have lived a more comfortable, but possibly less fulfilling, life.

Have a rescue plan. Knowing and planning for the worst contingency alleviates worry that can prevent you from making bold choices. My background is nursing. When I started my business, I simply wanted to match my modest nursing salary. What did I have to lose? Anytime I needed extra money to keep my enterprise afloat, I could work a few shifts at the hospital. Knowing I wouldn't sink entirely gave me courage.

Write your rescue plan. Look at your savings, earnings, and how long you'll need to float your enterprise before it generates adequate income. You're probably in better shape than you suspect. If not—you have two choices:

- Go all in anyway or
- Set a reasonable time period to succeed, then engage your rescue (just don't make it too early or too easy).

Either way, at least you've launched your ship.

CEO Secret 4: Solve Problems Quickly and Decisively

Top CEOs move so quickly they exhaust the people working with them, but speed is one of their success secrets. Not haphazard, as some might believe, fast-moving CEOs are constantly developing the concepts and principles that guide their rapid decision-making as they continuously strengthen the foundation of their enterprise.

Act like a CEO: Put the fundamentals in place so that you can implement creative and effective decisions. Then apply this problem-solving template and you'll leave people around you scratching their heads.

Define the situation. Define why it's important, the relevant facts, your goal in solving the problem, and the strategies you've already implemented.

List the people. Include family, consultants, coworkers, your housekeeper, your son's basketball coach—everyone who can help you solve the problem.

Sleep on it. The moments between sleep and consciousness are fertile ground for creative problem-solving. When you awake, the solution will often be waiting for you. Meditate on the issue or think about it while you exercise. I've often had to unwind from a yoga pose and pop out of the class to jot down a solution after having an "ah-ha" moment. When your conscious mind is quiet, your subconscious can work its magic.

Identify the necessary actions. Identify any actions you will personally take to resolve the problem. Look to your past successes and acknowledge that you have the inherent strengths. Identify the actions you will delegate. You don't have to do it all yourself. Top CEOs delegate extensively.

Evaluate the results. Apply what you learn to the next challenge that comes. Healthcare mistakes can be deadly, so when an incident occurred we always asked ourselves "What did we do wrong? What did we do right?" Evaluate each problem you solve and ask, "What can I learn that will help me in my future enterprises?"

An enterprising CEO never allows problems to thwart momentum. Resolve negative situations promptly and seek inventive ways to turn them into opportunities. I recently had to video-record one of our live training programs. I used that opportunity to revise the program, retrain the presenters, and demonstrate by example what and how to improve. Now we have not only a great new educational DVD to sell, but also a crack training team providing a vastly improved product.

As CEO, you're responsible for making decisions. No one can move or decide as quickly as you can. Accept that responsibility and keep the forward momentum going.

CEO Secret 5: Don't Be a Commodity

Top CEOs build businesses that are not easily duplicated. Ease of duplication creates commodities and a commodity business is the kiss of death. Water used to be a commodity until companies like Fiji and Perrier changed our perception. Then Coca-Cola and PepsiCo got involved, and water, available just about everywhere for free, outsells almost every other bottled drink at a high price.

My company sells an educational experience. We don't sell seminars, DVDs, or CDs, although those are the media we employ. Instead, we sell a lifelong relationship that includes mentoring and a reputation of being the pioneer and leader in the industry. Our ideas are often duplicated, but no one can duplicate our relationships, knowledge, or our twenty-six-year advantage.

No matter what you do or what your enterprising idea is, don't be a commodity. If you own a commodity business you'll go bankrupt, and if you work as a commodity for someone else you'll be poor.

To avoid becoming a commodity:

Build relationships. Be interested in others. Create genuine connections built on trust and caring, and you'll never be a commodity because you can never be duplicated. I've given one employee who is the "master of relationships" so many pay raises I've lost count. No matter the expertise, no one will ever duplicate her exceptional abilities and her loyalty. In return I get a higher quality of work, a higher level of commitment, and a willingness to help improve every company project.

Demonstrate trust. Trust has to be earned. Never promise what you can't deliver or you might not get a second chance. Instead, promise small and deliver big.

Go all in. Don't shrink into your chair and become invisible. If you're advancing through the corporate route, get in the middle of everything. I have employees who sit in the lunchroom staring at the clock until their lunch break is over. Others eat on the run to keep projects moving. Being involved doesn't mean being the last out the door each day or working endless overtime (although if you're always first out the door you'll end up last to be promoted). Being involved means caring about results, working productively, and letting others know of your involvement.

Strive to stand out. Demonstrate your ability to bring new ideas to a project or to your workplace. At our quarterly company brainstorming sessions some employees haven't spoken a word for years, others have "verbal diarrhea," and a treasured few constantly generate a flow of outstanding ideas. While you don't want to generate a torrent of mostly useless thoughts, you do want everyone to notice your contributions. It's easy to stand out when you pay attention and speak up.

CEO Secret 6: Don't Underprice Yourself

Top CEOs reject the common thinking that "if you drop your price you'll get the job" or "lower price equals higher sales." For twenty-six years people have said my products are too expensive—until they purchase and use them. If I had listened to the customers (and occasional staffer), I wouldn't be selling a $12,000 business system. I'd be selling a $60 textbook. Smart buyers understand that anything cheap can be expensive in the long run, and they will buy in to your enterprise as long as you provide value for the dollar.

As CEO of your life, your personal resources—time, energy, knowledge, integrity, and relationships—have a monetary value. If you value these resources too low, so will everyone else. People often say, "I can't control what I will get paid." Yes, you can. When my first hospital failed to offer what I knew I was worth after attaining my master's degree, I gave myself a pay raise by moving to another hospital.

When I still had to work overtime to pay my mortgage, I increased my pay again by starting my own business. Sometimes I think I'm still underpaid, but now I have no one to complain to except myself.

Place a high value on everything you know. In the information age, education doesn't come cheap and wisdom is gold.

Place a high value on everything you do. Outsource whatever you can. My first job every morning is to make sure my staff is doing as much of my work as I can delegate. That frees me to develop new tools, skills, and strategies for moving forward.

You may need to give up something to pursue your enterprise. Get your spouse to help with the dishes, the dinner, and carpool. Stop chairing every volunteer committee. Your time is one of your most precious assets. You only get twenty-four hours a day—choose to spend them wisely. If a project isn't supporting your enterprise, ask yourself how to drop it, delegate it, or find another way to accomplish it.

Become irreplaceable. As an employee, give your boss what he or she wants and more. Ultimately, no one is irreplaceable. I don't kid myself about that. If I went down in a plane wreck, the company would go on without me, although not exactly the same. You render yourself irreplaceable by making people think of you first for any project and feel they will profit measurably from your input, energy, and enterprising ideas.

Be original. Stamp your performance with originality so that you are not easily duplicated by a cheaper hire. Typists are commodities. Typists with the ability to organize, handle customers, keep a CEO on-target, and stay calm in the face of a crisis become executive assistants. Sales reps with great records stay longer than those with average sales. One really good idea a month might pay your bills, but having several will move you up the corporate ladder.

Ask for a pay raise. In my office I've had to give people pay raises because they underprice themselves. But don't wait for your boss to do that for you. Ask. My executive assistant quoted one of the highest salary requests I have ever encountered for that position. I weeded out the candidates who underpriced themselves, assuming they wouldn't work at the level I expected, and hired her at her asking price. It turned out she was worth it (but don't tell her I said that).

CEOs drive luxury cars, stay in luxury hotels, and dine at fine restaurants for a reason beyond personal gratification. They know that perception is important. I recommend you follow the old business adage: "to get ahead, dress like your boss's boss." The people immediately above you might not notice, but the people further up the ladder are the ones you want judging you against their own standard. Always present yourself and your work in a style that demonstrates value, and others will see you as priceless.

CEO Secret 7: Don't Overrate Networking

Sometimes I joke that time spent networking is time spent "not working." Enterprising CEOs are selective about where and with whom they network. You won't find them at your breakfast club meeting. CEOs research what they need, locate the source, and ask. They create a network of colleagues, clients, consultants, vendors, and acquaintances they can depend on to deliver anything from information to referrals.

I built my business on selective networking, but not through networking clubs, which can absorb time while distracting us from what we really need to accomplish. It's easy to convince yourself that heavy networking is productive when it's not. And you could be taking advice from people who mean well but are not qualified to give it. I'm always asking people I trust and respect, "Who do you know who . . . ?" I've gotten our company's marketing director, investment counselor, graphic design firm, and health insurance provider this way, not by trading business cards at a mixer.

Cast your net selectively. Don't confuse networking with socializing. Choose opportunities that put you in the middle of people who are more successful than yourself. Cultivate your network using your relationship skills to include the highest caliber professionals, the soundest minds, and the truest hearts.

Don't just hang around waiting to be introduced. Create your own introductions. I attended an *Inc.* conference for the top five thousand fastest-growing private companies in America. I mixed with CEOs and representatives from some of the country's top corporations. You can bet I had formulated different introductions for each of the different situations in which I found myself. Networking is sometimes a "once in your lifetime" opportunity—be prepared to make it pay off. Don't be a wallflower. If you don't feel comfortable introducing yourself to people, role-play with a friend and practice until you do. You have to step out to step up.

Give generously and demand reciprocation. Expect high performance from your network and reward performance. Say "thank you" with a note, flowers, a bottle of wine, or a nice lunch. Also, don't hesitate to cull out any person, business, or organization that repeatedly fails to perform.

Stay connected. Send handwritten notes, e-mails, and other thoughtful communications to create a lasting bond with clients, co-workers, and all members of your network. Something as simple as a "happy birthday" jotted on a card or a handwritten "thank you" instead of an e-mail will go far.

Strategically widen your net. Get in the habit of passing along names—your hair stylist, your plumber, your lawyer, your banker—not to just anyone, but selectively and with high praise. Their time is valuable too. They'll appreciate the selectivity as you would.

CEO Secret 8: Invest in Win-Win Relationships

Top CEOs make sure they're not the only ones gaining from their initiatives.

Initiate alignment. For any idea or project, look at what's in it for everyone—friends, families, coworkers, bosses. You'll get better participation and results when everyone benefits.

Initiate alliances. Create strategic alliances with people who can advance your career, and you theirs. You never know how you can help out a friend or colleague until you ask. People will appreciate your offer of help even if they refuse it.

In the corporate world, it never pays to alienate anyone. Ripples spread wide from rocks thrown in the lake. You never know who is aligned with whom. Never gossip and don't hesitate to say you're sorry (even when you're not). Treat everyone as an ally, even those who can't advance you. Never be condescending. Practice integrity with everyone at every level. It's always better to have allies than enemies.

Stay cool and clean. Avoid whiners, complainers, and the wrong crowd. Although the wrong crowd might appear popular, it won't be popular among the people who count. In the business world, avoid making your boss and administration the bad guys. Keep your hands and your nose clean—it'll pay off in the end.

CEO Secret 9: Compete Only with Yourself

Mushing a loaded dog sled across an Alaskan snowfield, I learned firsthand that it's true—if you're not the lead dog, the view from the rear never changes. And the rear is exactly where you'll be if you compete only with others.

To excel as an enterprising CEO you must be aware of competition, but don't allow that awareness to veer you off course. If you focus on your competition (someone brighter, richer, or better looking) you'll always be one step behind them. If you focus on your own enterprise and compete with your own best performance, you'll be the lead dog your competitors imitate, leaving them in the rear.

Be an innovator, not an imitator. Top CEOs know that what works today won't work tomorrow. That's why they focus on innovation. If you copy your competition today, you're already a step behind because he or she is already working on tomorrow.

Continually improve your education and skills. The world doesn't stand still and neither can you. The only way to stay ahead in this fast-paced era is to learn something new every day. Read books and magazines. Find a successful mentor to guide you. Research what you don't know. Hire consultants to fill in the gaps in your education or skill-set that you either don't have time for or don't want to learn. If you try to learn it all, you won't have time to do anything else. Hire specialists, consultants, and sharp employees.

Make advancements every year. Every CEO knows that a company advances, declines, or stagnates according to the expectations of its management team. When you expect to grow, and you put a growth plan in action, you'll see results. Greet each new year with an attainable, detailed growth plan that includes goals, strategies, and target dates.

Keep physically fit. Being a CEO is demanding. Life is demanding. To live life at its fullest and create an enterprise that makes you love getting out of bed every day, you have to feel your physical best. Your health is your most important asset. Put fitness at the top of your priorities. Schedule time at the gym. If you're physically fit, then you're more likely to be mentally fit. Schedule some quiet time. Innovative ideas emerge from silence.

Keep financially fit. A competitor once commented sarcastically that my clients pay for my big house, my big vacations, and my big smile. Of course they do. Any enterprise is profitable or it isn't an enterprise—it's a charity. The word "profit" stems from a Latin word meaning "advancement or improvement." As CEO, you must expect to profit from every investment.

Create an income and spending plan. Make a budget and stick to it. Keep the cash flow positive. You owe it to yourself and your family to be financially fit, and being free from financial worry allows you to pursue your enterprise with passion.

CEO Secret 10: Get Your Hands Dirty

I joke that I'm a working CEO, a style that makes things happen. Successful CEOs get their hands dirty. All great chefs start by working in the kitchen. You can't cook from behind your desk, so get up, get out, and chop some onions.

The best leaders lead by example. If you get down in the trenches, instead of always standing on the sidelines giving orders, it is easier to convince others to fall in with you. And you'll demonstrate the results you expect. You don't have to pack every box that ships out, mail every invoice, or fill every jelly donut for a day. Be in the space; demonstrate that you understand the job that each employee is doing. Ask questions and listen to the answers. Be willing to work.

In coaching women for twenty-six years, I've observed that for many people the enterprising vision is the easy part. Committing to the dirty details that convert that vision into reality is tough. It often involves early mornings, late nights, working weekends, and carrying out the trash. If you don't do the dirty work or have someone do it for you, your enterprise will fail.

Clean the kitchen. In my company, everybody takes a turn at kitchen duty. In my household, everybody is expected to clean up their own messes and pitch in at meals. As CEO, you have to set the example—then demand that everyone follow it. You're responsible for your gains and your mistakes. Responsible people gain respect, so clean up your own messes and be responsible.

Make the coffee. The first one in makes the coffee, right? That's responsibility on a small scale. A CEO shoulders responsibility for getting many projects started. You show how it's done, set the pace, then offload some of that responsibility so you can pioneer the next project. Check in and have a cup of coffee now and then to make sure the standard is being upheld.

Turn off the lights. The last person out locks up. Someone has to sign off that a project is finalized with all the t's crossed. Enterprising CEOs don't take this for granted. The best ideas can bomb when final details are overlooked. It's your name on the door—so be sure the right people are focused on those details.

CEO Secret 11: Make Perpetual Lists

CEOs have assistants to remind them what to do. Like executive assistants, lists can save you hours of fumbling and head-scratching. Lists keep you organized and prevent wasted time going back for an item you forgot.

I maintain a perpetual grocery list on my computer, which I simply update and print out when it's time to shop. I keep a list of travel items to pack no matter where I'm going. I also keep a list of future business ideas so I won't forget them. Which of your routines would benefit from being perpetualized on a grab-it-and-go list?

List the steps. Anything you do repeatedly that requires specific steps—from shopping for the kids' school supplies to publishing a newsletter—can benefit from a checklist. Break it down into the smallest steps. Update it as you go, adding, deleting, and recategorizing items as necessary.

List the people skills. How can you possibly remember all the aptitudes and the expertise of every person in your network? It's easy when you have a list. List everybody you know alphabetically. Beside their names, write down what they do professionally, the organizations they belong to, their pastime interests, and any other skills, abilities, and talents they have. Every time you learn something new about a person, add it to your list. What a priceless resource you'll have!

List the essentials. For any situation that requires take-alongs—from picnicking to running a meeting—list every item necessary or even desirable to make the event successful. You can always elect to eliminate something on the list, but if it's listed, at least you have the option before you go rather than when it's too late.

CEO Secret 12: Put Systems to Work for You

CEOs like to spend their time creating, so they're adept at systemizing routine tasks.

Anything you do repeatedly can be systemized so that others can do it. Systemize everything, and don't reinvent the wheel every day (only on the days it really, really needs it).

Ask "how can I do it faster?" Write down all the steps you take to accomplish a routine task. Don't cheat; put in absolutely everything. Now look at all that work. Which steps can you eliminate or reduce and get the same result? If you can systemize your task, work so that it's reproducible; you can delegate it, which means more time to do more important things.

Ask "how can I do it easier?" What tools would facilitate this task? When you have to pound a lot of nails, you want a heavy hammer. Better yet, a pneumatic nail gun. Or would a staple gun work better? The right tools can smooth any process.

Ask "how can I do it cheaper?" A CEO's time is the most costly in the entire company. I've known high-level employees who claim it's faster to do things themselves rather than delegate and train. Using their high-dollar time on tasks that should be delegated is costly to their companies. What can you effectively systemize and delegate that would result in a better allocation of time and money?

Create templates. E-mails, letters, forms, and other documents that must be created or updated frequently can be systemized. For any new document, first review what already exists. Then copy, adapt, and pull from previous efforts.

Automate online processes. Use the tools that make your Internet use faster and easier. Beyond book-marking your favorite site, rent a Web-savvy geek for a day to show you how to automate searches, postings, news you need, and e-mail.

Make it a habit to look for ways to systemize processes. As CEO, you can accomplish more in less time with less stress by using available systems or creating your own. If you systemize one process a week, think of all the vacation time you'll earn, or the time you'll have for other parts of your enterprise.

Take the Driver's Seat

You can be successful at many endeavors. Even though we all have to do things that are not our top favorites, successful self-development lies in selecting and focusing on the enterprising activities you like to do and continually improving what you do well. People often think I go after all kinds of ideas, and I'll admit to constantly aiming for higher levels, but over the years I've rejected many ideas because they didn't meet my criteria for an enterprising life, a life of choice.

Top CEOs like Oprah Winfrey and Donald Trump are masters of selection and masters of enterprise. Use my Twelve CEO Secrets, apply the CEO strength of enterprise to whatever you want to accomplish as a result, and you'll always be in the driver's seat. You'll choose your own destination, make the road rules, and cash the big checks. Everyone will yearn to discover your secrets and replicate your success.

Life, the grandest enterprise of all, is as thrilling a ride as you want to make it—and you're the CEO in charge. So act like it today and you'll rise to the top tomorrow.

Vickie L. Milazzo, RN, MSN, JD

VICKIE L. MILAZZO, RN, MSN, JD, is the founder and owner of Vickie Milazzo Institute. She is credited by *The New York Times* with pioneering a new specialty practice of nursing—legal nurse consulting—in 1982. *Inc.* recognized Vickie as one of the nation's Top 10 Entrepreneurs and named her company one of the Top 5000 Fastest-Growing Private Companies in America. She is the author of the *Wall Street Journal* bestseller, *Inside Every Woman: Using the 10 Strengths You Didn't Know You Had to Get the Career and Life You Want Now* (currently in its sixth printing).

Vickie L. Milazzo, RN, MSN, JD
Vickie Milazzo Institute
5615 Kirby Drive, Suite 425
Houston, Texas 77005-2448
Phone: 800.880.0944
E-mail: mail@LegalNurse.com
www.LegalNurse.com
www.InsideEveryWoman.com

❧

BREAKING THROUGH TO PASSION

Pat McKelvey

It seems that all the success mentors I have seen, heard, or read experienced great poverty and hardship before they eventually achieved great fame and fortune. They fought valiantly to overcome these circumstances with the tools they were teaching us, leading to the message that "If I could achieve all this coming from such a background, you can too."

It gradually dawned on me that they had succeeded not so much "in spite of" their challenges, but "because of" them. Their lives were extremely uncomfortable, and their souls strove to relieve that discomfort, fueling their persistence in their great efforts and creativity.

I, on the other hand, had the "handicap of happiness." Raised by loving, upper-middle-class parents who told me I could be and do anything I wanted, I approached the world as if it were a lavish "smorgasbord" (I *am* one-quarter Norwegian). I had (and still have) many interests, and love to learn new things. Add to this mix the "curse of competence," and I was perfectly set up for my trial-and-error career path. I was good at many things and it seems like I tried most of them!

Instead of overcoming obstacles, as I heard the success mentors talk about, I seemed to turn my blessings into barriers. Because I had a wonderful high school chemistry teacher, I majored in chemistry in college. My senior year, after I had completed my major and been accepted into one of the top five graduate schools for chemistry in the country, I took my first sociology course. I *loved* it! But to change my major and life's direction at that point would have required three more years of college. So I continued on the path of least resistance—chemistry. Little did I know how much more than three years this decision would cost me later in life!

At a challenging graduate school, I aced the courses and other PhD requirements, then settled into three years of research required for my thesis. It was unbelievably boring. I used to say that it was like cooking without getting to eat what I made.

After a turbulent relationship with a gorgeous (older) student in one of the undergraduate classes for which I was a teaching assistant, I fell in love with a post-doctoral student in my department. When he completed his work there and moved 2,000 miles away to get a teaching position, I followed him. I realized later that a big part of my decision was based on two things that were not part of a solid foundation for a relationship: 1) I was on the rebound from my first love, and 2) it was a good excuse to drop out of the PhD program, settling for a master's degree as a "consolation prize" for all the academic work I had done. I could never have disappointed my parents after all their years of financial and moral support by leaving merely because I was no longer interested in the work. I knew that the "M-r-s" I would get from marriage was the only thing they would value as much as a "P-h-D."

A marriage founded on such a basis could hardly be expected to be very successful, and indeed it was not. After six months, I wanted out. But he said he would change, and for a while things were better. So I stayed with him for seven years. After all, we had a twenty-seven-acre farm with horses, dogs, cats, and even chickens—a childhood dream come true!

Of course, as I realized many years later, the problem was not about him. I had created it all from my ineffective, security-based mental conditioning. I was not very happy for most of those seven years, and I probably would have accepted living at such a low level of happiness because I didn't know that anything better was possible.

But an act of grace saved me from this uninspiring life—my husband got a university teaching job hundreds of miles away, and suggested that I stay at my job and keep the farm until he found out if he got tenure. When he left, a friend moved in as my roommate, and I had so much more fun with her than I had had with him that I knew I would never move to his new location. Through marriage counseling, we ended the marriage amicably, and remain friends to this day. (He is even more friendly with my parents, who are geographically closer to him than I am.)

Career-wise, my life was not going much better because, of course, it was all a reflection of the same conditioning. Fed up with chemistry, my first job out of graduate school was as a secretary and I *loved* it! But then a company to which I had applied for a similar position offered me a job as a chemist (apparently they actually do read those resumes!). The pay was so much higher than my secretarial pay that I decided to at least to talk to them. I discovered that unlike my university research, industrial chemistry actually involved work that affected people directly—through the products developed in the lab. I gave up a job working with people to take a job working with chemicals so that we could more quickly earn the down payment on that farm.

I had a series of five jobs as a chemist in fourteen years, always thinking that it was the boss or the projects or the company that I didn't like. I quit one job because they wouldn't give me two months off for a tour of Europe. That was one of the few instances during that time period when I chose in favor of my heart's desire instead of what seemed practical or reasonable or sensible from all my conditioning about what it meant to be successful.

I had totally forgotten that I hadn't wanted to be a chemist at all and had gotten lured into it by the money! Then I sat next to an amazing woman on a plane. I traveled a lot for business, and made it a policy to not talk to the people next to me because I always had reading I needed to do. I didn't want to risk having them take up my whole flight talking to me! (As I write this now, from my totally shifted way of life, I am astonished that I could have ever been so averse to talking with people, which is now my greatest joy!)

But the ever-supportive, loving Universe/God/Cosmic Consciousness was really looking out for me this time! The woman was wearing unusual clothing, including a flamboyant hat that she struggled to put into the overhead compartment. She was reading a fascinating-looking book on Native American spirituality, and the flight was only an hour long. My curiosity was piqued, and I couldn't resist starting a conversation.

It turned out that she was a career counselor! "When the student is ready, the teacher appears." We set an appointment for me to meet with her, and my life was forever changed.

It did not take us long to realize that I was in the wrong career. But then something much more amazing happened. During the brief time I was her career counseling client, she "experienced her enlightenment," as it is expressed in the Eastern Vedic tradition which she had been studying for years. She shifted from career counseling to spiritual counseling, starting with Kundalini yoga. As a very left-brained, analytical person, I would never have come near such a "far out" character if I had met her just a few weeks after I did. But having gotten to know, trust, and respect her as a career counselor, I stayed along for the ride. And what a ride it was!

As her student, I learned enormous amounts about Eastern spirituality and had amazing experiences of blissful energy. I quit my job (and career) as a chemist immediately after the one and only time I was ever drawn into spontaneous meditation at work. It was a vision of a tunnel with light at the end, which my teacher had told us was a sign that God would take care of us.

It came right before my boss called me into his office to tell me that I would no longer be doing the half of my job I enjoyed—customer service—because they needed me to do the other half full-time. That other half was lab work, which was what I had disliked so much about graduate school! Very calmly, and very unlike my normal response to such a situation, I said that that would not be acceptable to me, and I would like to be transferred to a position that was 100 percent customer service. What a blessing that the meditation had given me the courage and confidence to follow the guidance of my Higher Self, against all the fears of my Conditioned Mind!

My employer was not able to find a position that would satisfy me, so amazingly enough, I was given three months' severance pay when I left the company. God definitely did take care of me as promised in that meditation!

Now that I was free of the shackles of a job I had never really liked, in a field of study that had lost its appeal somewhere during my college years, I embarked on much more intense spiritual study, as well as a potpourri of jobs/careers. My spiritual teacher was no longer a career counselor, so I began my trial-and-error phase of career choice. Many of the jobs involved sales, marketing, and public relations. My favorite, which did not pay anywhere near enough to live on, was as a guide on bus tours of the area for visiting convention and tour groups. I loved talking to people who were on these bus tours because they wanted to learn new things and to have fun. This was a clue to my true calling, which I did not realize until many years later.

My only job during this period that really amounted to anything was as a financial planner. I had always been good with numbers and interested in learning more about investing. This job also allowed me to talk to people about something very important to them—their financial growth and security.

I also got started in network marketing, seeing the beauty of its design back in the 1980s before most people appreciated it at all. I loved the fact that it involved working with people to promote their personal and financial growth, and that those higher up in the compensation plan were rewarded for helping those below them. How unlike all the corporate jobs I had had, where some of my bosses had stolen my ideas and backstabbed their colleagues and employees. And yet many people said that multi-level marketing (as it was called then) was a "pyramid scheme"! There is nothing more pyramidal than the corporate structure, where the only way to great wealth is to climb over coworkers to reach the top of that pyramid! In network marketing, someone can easily earn more than all the people above him or her in the compensation plan. How egalitarian!

Even with all those benefits, the greatest benefit of network marketing, as Jim Rohn said many years ago, is the person you have to become to achieve the success you want.

At last I was launched into the areas of personal and spiritual growth that would lead to my greatest passions. I took the est training in the 1980s (now morphed into the Landmark Forum). Then I did other personal and spiritual growth programs, and began to read almost nothing except books and articles on these subjects.

In 2000 I received an invitation in the mail to attend an event where Robert Allen would be talking about his new book, *Multiple Streams of Income*. The offer of a free copy of one of his earlier books for attending, plus the chance to meet a famous wealth-maker in person, brought me there. It turned out that the event was really to promote his new Protégé Program, where for a few thousand dollars we could receive teleclasses, books, and tapes on all the areas of wealth-building expertise he had amassed over the years. I was enthralled by his presence. He talked with each person who was interested in becoming a protégé individually, and seemed to really care about their success and happiness. I signed up.

I learned a lot about real estate, Internet marketing, infopreneuring (information marketing), and a little about the stock market. I went to several of his wealth retreats and talked to him in person again and again. I attended his very small seminars on Persuasion and Inner Wealth, which were about the psychological, sociological, and spiritual aspects of success. I resonated with these the most strongly. And I always loved the chance to talk to him in person. After a few years he even recognized and remembered me!

It was because of the trust and respect I had for him that I got on a teleclass he recommended that was being given by a relatively unknown (in 2003, in the United States), personal and spiritual growth trainer, T. Harv Eker. I was blown away by what Harv said about our "money blueprint" and "financial thermostat." He put into words all that I had subconsciously felt during my years of working hard but not being very happy or financially successful. I was conditioned for mediocrity! Even with all the benefits I had had—intelligence, excellent education, loving and supportive parents, empathy and appreciation for others—I was never going to achieve greatness in anything if my subconscious was following its instructions to keep me below the psychological ceiling created by my conditioning!

I immediately called to register for his "Millionaire Mind Intensive," being given for the first time outside of Canada, in Los Angeles, in May 2003. It was, as he promised, a life-changing event. I could see that he had a very powerful teaching, based on years of spiritual study that bridged the worlds of spiritual/personal growth and financial success. I had first experienced that with Robert Allen, and now, with Harv's Peak Potentials seminars and camps, I was getting it in an incredibly powerful way.

I went on to take almost all of Peak Potentials' courses, including Guerilla Business School, The World's Greatest Marketing Seminar, Wealth and Wisdom, Master of Influence, Never Work Again, Seminar of the Century, and the most amazing programs, Enlightened Warrior Training Camp and Wizard Training Camp. I also was a volunteer staff member at the first Ultimate Leadership Camp held in California in September 2006. All of Peak Potentials' courses are very experiential, but the camps are *intensely* experiential, to very great effect.

The Peak Potentials course that changed my life the most, though, was Life Directions. If there was ever anyone who needed that, I was that one! Trial and error had not really produced the results I had hoped and longed for. My spiritual life had become focused on the question of "Why am I here on this planet at this time?" I desperately wanted to discover my calling, my purpose, my destiny.

I had, of course, read many of the excellent books on that subject, but somehow they had not been able to break through my very strong resistance/conditioning. Life Directions was brilliantly structured to start with those sorts of processes (what you enjoyed doing as a child, what people say you are good at, etc.) and use them in very creative and effective ways to reveal each person's unique path that fulfills his or her heart's desires.

It is very interesting that what I discovered to be my calling at Life Directions was something I had been getting clues about in my life for months before that course. Now, in writing this, it seems like they had been there from the beginning. That darn conditioning, which for most of my life I didn't even know existed, was acting like blinders to keep me from recognizing those clues. As Wayne Dyer said many years ago, "believing is seeing," not the other way around, as we were taught. We can only see what fits our belief systems, and I was a prime example of that.

I had noticed, in the months before the seminar, that people—some of whom I knew well, and some of whom I had just met—were telling me about serious and often very personal problems in their lives. I was coming up with things to say that really helped them see these situations in a better light or to see a solution for themselves or other outcomes that they found very valuable. I even experienced this on the flight to Los Angeles for the seminar; someone I met on the plane received a very painful phone call from his brother as we were talking after the flight. I came up with an analogy that got him through his tears into joy. Another blessing—and clue—from God/Universe!

So I was not as resistant as I might have been otherwise to find out in Life Directions that my calling is to be a coach. I recognized that I had been dismissing all the earlier evidence because my conditioning said that it would be too expensive and take too long to become accredited as a coach. After all, I had "wasted" my life up until now in education for a career that I knew in my senior year in college that I did not want, and then when I left chemistry, in a series of trial-and-error career choices. Wasn't it too late now to go "back to school" to start another career?

I trusted Harv and his course enough to at least ask some of the volunteer coaches working at Life Directions the cost in time and money for them to become coaches. They told me, as I feared, that it was years, and thousands of dollars. And then I experienced another blessing when I talked to someone else because I knew her from the year before when she "just happened" to sit next to me on the flight home from Guerilla Business School. (I put that in quotation marks, because I truly believe there are no coincidences.) At that time she talked to me about the American Seminar Leaders Association, of which she was the head, and which I had no interest in joining. But like my earlier teacher whom I met on a plane, she was so interesting, warm, and loving (and was wearing a beautiful hat!) that I was drawn to her on a personal level. When I asked her about coaching, a year after that first meeting, she told me that she had just started a coaching training program! She said that it was better, shorter, and less expensive than other programs currently available. When I took her training, I discovered how true that was.

Like my earlier spiritual teacher, June totally turned my life around—not just with her coaching training, but also with her loving and supportive mentorship. I became a coach for Peak Potentials and had the incredible blessing, joy, and fulfillment of traveling the path of personal and spiritual growth with my highly motivated clients. It was also a great blessing when they told me that my insights, support, and loving way of holding them accountable to themselves allowed them to do things and achieve levels of success that they could not have done by themselves.

June astutely encouraged me to focus on financial coaching because of my background in financial planning, as well as the fact that I was a mortgage loan agent at the time. It was very rewarding to see how much difference it could make to someone when I shared the things that I took for granted about financial management, but which they either never had the interest or opportunity to learn. These were things like:

1. You can always negotiate with a credit card company, and will often get results such as a decreased interest rate, increased credit limit, and decreased or eliminated annual fee. If you don't get what you want the first time, call back at a different time; different customer service agents may give you different responses.

2. Your credit score is very important in determining not just what kind of home loan you can get, but also what interest rate you get on your credit cards, whether you are considered for high-level jobs, and whether you will be accepted as a resident in some exclusive apartment complexes. There are many ways to legally increase your credit score, some of which are obvious (like paying your bills on time), and some of which are closely-guarded secrets of the credit bureaus who do the calculations. One of my favorites regarding the latter (because it so easy to do) is that if you pay more than the minimum payment on your credit cards

on which you carry a balance, this will improve your score, *even if you only pay $1 more per payment!* Another lesser-known way that is somewhat more difficult to do is to keep all your credit card balances below half of their credit limit. Calling to increase your credit limit, as in number one (above) can help you do this.

3. There is a lot of concern about the negative effect that checking your credit has on your score, much of it without basis. For example, multiple requests within a thirty-day period usually only count as one request, if the bureaus can see that they are all the same type of credit and can therefore assume that you are shopping for credit for a single purchase (such as a home or car). And requests for a credit report do not affect your score at all if they are made through certain programs such as those designed to monitor your accounts for identity theft. Always ask the provider of those programs whether this is the case, as they sometimes automatically request a report every thirty days.

4. Do not automatically close a credit account when it is paid off, especially if it is an older account. One of the factors used to determine credit scores is the length of time you have had credit, and closing an account will decrease this. Also, it will decrease your available credit, thereby increasing your credit balance to credit limit ratio (see number two, above). However, if you will be tempted to use this credit unwisely, and get yourself into further credit problems, it is worth the short-term cost to your credit score to close the account.

In spite of my strong financial background, I was still very nervous about doing my first coaching call. I was reviewing my extensive materials and notes from June's training, and feeling like I would never get it all "down" enough so that I could feel confident taking another person's life in my hands. It was at that time when God/Universe once more gave me a great blessing. I was calling my first client to schedule our first call, and she either misunderstood the purpose of my call or was in so much distress that it didn't matter what I was calling about, because she immediately started telling me her very serious financial problems and pleading for help. My empathy and desire to be of assistance (as well as the knowledge I had of financial matters) came immediately to the fore, and I discovered on the spot that I really did know how to coach! She was greatly helped by that call, and I was never nervous about another coaching call again!

This is a very good example of something that my success mentors had often spoken about, but which has always been hard for me to put into action—the only way past fear is through it. Courage is not the lack of fear, it is the willingness to act in spite of fear. The best way to eliminate fear is through action taken in the direction of that which is feared. In this case, I was pushed into action by a friendly, supportive Universe/God because I had not been able or willing to take that action on my own.

Robert Allen talks a lot about overcoming fear. He asks how we get through the wall of fear that we all have, which is created by our critical mind, our loved ones, the media, and so many other influences in our environments. He gives the example that a ship in the harbor is safe, but that's not what it's made for. What if we looked for how we can get what we want instead of why we can't get it? Both answers are there. Which one do we want?

My coaching has broadened to include more than just financial management because it became clear very quickly that in addition to properly handling our debt, we must increase our income if we are to achieve our dreams. Overcoming fear is a big part of finding new sources of income or of increasing the income from our current sources. It goes back to the financial thermostat on which Harv bases his Millionaire Mind Intensive and his best-selling book *Secrets of the Millionaire Mind*. Our thermostat is set at the level at which we are comfortable. To increase our wealth, we must raise the thermostat out of the comfort zone into the fear zone. Around the borders of our comfort zone lie our fears, like prison guards, keeping us in. One of my coaching clients thought of the following way of expressing this idea after one of our calls, and he has posted it where he sees it every day: "On the other side of fear is success."

My studies of how to motivate ourselves to move through that fear soon led me to the amazing work on *passion* done by Janet and Chris Attwood. It made sense out of the study done years ago that the 5 percent of the Yale graduating class who had written goals made more money after twenty years than the other 95 percent combined. I could never understand why that made so much difference, so I could never make myself write down goals. Now I see that goals/dreams/desires/passions are the accelerator that can override our brakes of fear, apathy, and lack of focus.

After reading Chris and Janet's breakthrough book *The Passion Test: the Effortless Path to Discovering Your Destiny*, I began to see signs of the importance of passion everywhere. For example, in *Success Built to Last: Creating a Life that Matters,* by Jerry Porras, Stewart Emery, and Mark Thompson, interviews with hundreds of successful people from all areas of life and around the world showed that what they all had in common was their passion for what they were doing. I started seeing passion mentioned all around me, such as in this quote from filmmaker George Lucas: "You have to find something that you love enough to be able to take risks, jump over the hurdles, and break through the brick walls that are always going to be placed in front of you. If you don't have that kind of feeling for what it is you're doing, you'll stop at the first giant hurdle" (courtesy of Cynthia Kersey, author of *Unstoppable*). Cynthia adds: "Becoming unstoppable requires passion. Without it, as George Lucas said above, you'll stop at the first giant hurdle."

The Passion Test is a deceptively simple and exceedingly powerful way to discover your passions, and hence your destiny. It includes the steps that will enable you to follow the "effortless path" to living your passions and destiny. After listening to Janet and Chris go through the test with volunteers on a teleclass, then reading their book and taking their "Discover Your Destiny" seminar, I used their approach with all my coaching clients. Some of them told me that after years of working on their personal and spiritual growth, this was the missing link that allowed all the other parts to come together. This is because the Passion Test gives us clarity and focus in our lives—two critical elements that most people will say they are missing.

Clients experienced miracles in manifesting their desires, a topic that has become very well-known since the phenomenal success of the DVD *The Secret.* This is only appropriate because Janet and Chris were very instrumental in helping Rhonda Byrne with this project, and are very attuned to this ancient and powerful law in all their own work.

I became so passionate about the Passion Test and its ability to help people with what had once been an all-consuming issue in my life—the discovery of my purpose and my destiny—that I also took their first training to be a Certified Passion Test Facilitator. I wanted to be able to more effectively bring this extremely important, groundbreaking work to my clients and others who are open to receiving the value it provides.

Openness here, as in all things, is key. As I realized in looking back at my own life path, we are constantly receiving messages to help us find our way. All that is asked of us is to *be open* to what the events in our lives can teach us. As we learned at Wizard Training Camp, "everything happens for a reason, and that reason is there to serve me."

I firmly believe that each of us was put here with a purpose, a mission, a destiny, and that that destiny is to travel our own unique, personal path, which will eventually lead us to self-actualization, enlightenment, self-realization, oneness with God/Universe, or whatever words your belief system is most comfortable with.

It is hard to change once you have become successful in a career. It could easily feel like all the years you spent preparing for and moving up in that career would be wasted if you left it. You might even feel like you were "sinking to the bottom" instead of "rising to the top" if you start over in a new field.

But if you stick to a path that you entered upon to fulfill the dreams of others or because you didn't fully understand your own heart's desires, you will leave this life with your music left unsung, your unique gift not given. It is my passion, my gift, and my mission to prevent that tragedy from happening to as many people as possible.

To paraphrase Dickens: It is the best of times, it is the worst of times. It is the best because of the incredible number and variety of personal and spiritual growth opportunities and tools available to us. It is the worst because our need for them is greater than ever. A world on the edge of catastrophe and collapse calls out for all that each of us can contribute, and the value of our contribution increases dramatically as our level of self-awareness and self-growth increases, and as our alignment with our passions and purpose increases.

Another reason this is an incredible time to be alive is the convergence of different fields of knowledge toward the same ultimate truth. Those in science, spirituality, philosophy, psychology, and even business are all coming to recognize certain fundamental truths:

1. Everything is energy.
2. Our thoughts create our reality.

From very early in my life, I have longed for this time when the realization of the ultimate truth is approached, like the hub of a wheel, from all points on the perimeter of the wheel. If you look at each spoke of the wheel independently, it appears to be leading in a different direction from all the others. But that is only because each is starting from a different point, and to reach the same endpoint, it has to head in the unique direction that will take it to the "hub" of truth, just as each of us travels a different path to reach the same ultimate truth. At last, each field of knowledge has gotten close enough to the hub to see the other fields approaching as well. Cooperation and collaboration are beginning to replace competition.

After all I have experienced and studied, I am convinced that overcoming the conditioning of our mind is the most important thing we can do to progress spiritually, psychologically, socially, and financially. I continue to study and explore manifestation, the Law of Attraction, and the other universal laws to which *The Secret* was such a fine introduction. If we are not always growing, we are dying. We must always strive to be "rising to the top" even though we will never reach it. If we are following our passions and living our destiny, that journey itself will be our joy and our reward.

Pat McKelvey

PAT MCKELVEY is a financial/spiritual/destiny coach. After graduating at the top of her large high school class, she continued to be very successful as a student in college, and working toward a PhD in chemistry, only to realize after almost three years in graduate school that chemistry wasn't her passion. She became a financial planner and mortgage loan agent, and embarked on a long spiritual path served by Eastern and Western spiritual and personal growth teachers, always seeking her purpose for being here. When she discovered her destiny, she became passionate about helping others discover theirs.

Pat McKelvey
Destiny Coach
Certified Passion Test Facilitator
P.O. Box 1846
Pacifica, CA 94044-6846
Phone: 650.994.1330
877.327.1066 (Voice Mail)
www.yourdestinycoach.com
coaching@yourdestinycoach.com

ARE YOU LIVING IN THE SUCCESS STATE? FIND YOUR MOST POTENT QUOTIENT FOR SUCCESS

Judith Shinoda Berry

Success is a state of being. It is not a destination. Success is in a constant state of flux that once reached, does not automatically freeze in a fixed position. Instead, the "Success State" must be maintained. The *Success State* is achieved when all parts of the self are in alignment with the Infinite Self. This alignment occurs when communication lines are open and operating in an active, flowing state within the self. It is maintained through a unique awareness we call intuition.

What is intuition? Intuition is a voice that comes to the conscious mind through the body. It is an important part of us that most people ignore. It is a universal connection to all things in the universe. Intuition is not a psychic ability as some people think. It is a type of communication within the self that is geared toward keeping us in the Success State. So, to ignore our intuition is to ignore our most powerful success guidance system.

I had come to a crossroads in my career choices when I heard the inner voice of my True Self for the first time. When I heard it, I went into an emotional shock. It felt like lightening striking me from behind. It did not creep up on me nor did it touch me softly. Instead, it shot through my mind and freed me from my family's definition of success.

The intuitive part of me cried out, "Wait! If you choose the conventional career path, you will make more money. You will have a beautiful house and a three-car garage for the vehicles you will be driving. You will also have a great job title and a position of distinction. You will be very successful and at the top of your field. More importantly, you will have the 401(k) retirement plan you have been dreaming of when you retire."

Wow! I was excited when I heard these words from my inner voice. Everything that I dreamed of in terms of financial success and career had been defined. What more could I want? My family would be proud of me. I would feel proud of myself. What a fantastic feeling of pride it gave me when I thought about it!

However, my voice of intuition told me there was another choice. The voice said, "But, there is another path you can follow. On this path you will have so much fun and meet highly interesting people. You will be very happy with what you do. You will stand in front of large audiences of people who will travel miles to hear what you have to say. The joy that radiates from your body will heal those who come to see you. The love experienced with you will change lives. Happiness and laughter will be a part of your daily existence. You will be blessed more than you know. Sometimes your job will be dangerous, but you will not be harmed or destroyed. When you conquer your fears, those emotions will leave you and you can travel the world. But once you make your decision, you cannot go back to your other choice."

The idea that I could never go back to my other career choice worried me. I began to do a comparative analysis of my two choices. They were both so different. I could not fathom what the second choice was about. Why did I have these two entirely different paths to choose from? They made no sense at the time. I did not know what to do. The first thought I had was, "This is crazy. Why would I ever think of putting myself in danger for a job? Why would I choose to talk to large audiences of people who will travel to see me? I don't even like standing up and introducing myself to a group of people."

It has been many years since I made the choice to find out who I am. Every day that I wake up and every evening that I fall off to sleep, shows me a new version of myself. Some days I really love myself for the choice I made back then. There are days that I laugh and days that I cry. And then I wonder again, who am I now?

Intuition is the voice of truth. It is not designed to create guilt in us because that is the job of the ego. Intuition, if understood properly, tells each of us the truth in a language that we create within ourselves and interpret through our body. Intuition is our truth and lie detector. That is why we know when we are living in the light of truth and in the Success State. When our intuition detects a lie, we feel the warning in the body like that feeling deep in the pit of our stomach that tells us when we are off course.

Success is different for everyone. The success quotient is unique to each individual. How is our success quotient determined? To begin with, we are souls with a unique life purpose and destiny. Every person's life purpose is also unique with each lifetime. No matter how many lifetimes we spend on this planet, we will have a different life purpose each time. If our purpose for living is different, then our destiny will also be different. That is why there is no carbon copy of our soul or spirit. We evolve with each experience even if it is buying groceries at a supermarket. The number of customers and employees, the variations of merchandise or stock amounts and the like constantly change with every visit. And so it is the same with our life's purpose. It is different in every lifetime.

The first three steps to living in the Success State are comprised of establishing three factors to *determine our unique potent quotient for success:*

1. Our True Self
2. Our Life Destiny
3. Our Life's Purpose

There are many unique ways to manifest the Life Path from starting Point A at the True Self and traveling through our lifetime to end Point B at our Life Destiny. Each of the following Figures 1–4 illustrate a different approach to the amount of time and effort used to reach the end point of our Life Destiny.

Point A in Figures 1–4 represents our True Self, our beginning point at any point in our life. When we know our Life's Purpose or Life Destiny at ending Point B, our Life Path becomes visible to us consciously.

Figure 1. The Enlightened Being. This is the intuitively aware being that is always present on the Life Path. People who live as Enlightened Beings live intuitively in the Success State and know that the shortest distance between two points is a straight line. They can avoid taking tangents to learn life lessons or falling off the Life Path by living consciously in the moment. They soar through life in happiness and bliss without having to incur the distress and regret most other approaches people choose to experience on their journey. As you see, this is the quickest, easiest, and most direct approach in achieving your Life's Purpose and Destiny.

Figure 2. The Positive Being. This Conscious Being lives life intuitively aware while choosing to learn life lessons along the way. These people experience tangents on the Life Path, but consciously recognize what they are learning as they go. They are happy souls who chuckle to themselves instead of losing their balance while they are learning a life lesson. Eventually they learn to straighten the curves in the Life Path by becoming the path.

Figure 3. The Difficult Being. This Being moves forward on his or her Life Path, but chooses to learn the "hard way." People like this create a rhythmic pattern of successes and failures that tend to feel something like, "ten steps forward and two steps back, eight steps forward and one step back, twelve steps forward and three steps back," and so on. Although they make more progress moving forward than they make falling back, it is uncertain if they will find out if they will achieve their Destiny and Life's Purpose in the end. They either fall short or barely reach their life goals and Destiny.

Figure 4. The Avoidant Being. Avoidant Beings are lost on their Life Path. Whether it is by conscious choice or unconscious living, they seemingly refuse the path of least resistance at every offering. These beings create disharmony if they experience success, sending them tumbling backward out of control until they "hit bottom" so they must start all over again.

Various Approached to
Achieving One's Destiny on the Life Path

Legend:
A = The True Self
B = Life Destiny
The Line - Life Time

Fig. 1   **The Enlightened Being:**
          Intuitively aware and always present on the Life Path.

A _____ B

Fig 2.   **The Positive Being**
          Conscious and exploring lessons on the Life Path.

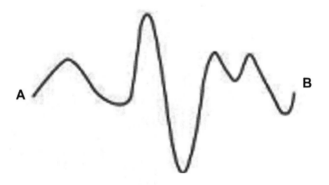

Various Approaches to
Achieving One's Destiny on the Life Path

Legend:
A = True Self
B = Life Destiny
The Line = Life Time

Fig. 3   **The Difficult One**
Moves forward but learns lessons the hard way on the
Life Path

Fig. 4   **The Avoidant Being**
Wastes time and makes little progress on the Life Path.

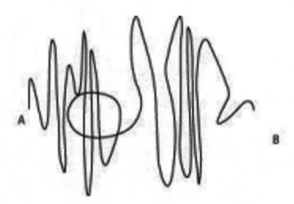

When we look at the differences between Figures 1 through 4 we can see that the straight line approach of the Enlightened Being in Figure 1 saves the most time and effort in his or her life's journey. The straighter the line, the more direct the person is on the path. Enlightened Beings are free to choose whatever they wish to experience with the extra time and energy at their disposal.

Yet, an occasional tangent is sometimes helpful to learn a lesson, especially if it is invested well. The Positive Being in Figure 2 listens closely to his or her intuition and decides whether to take the tangent or continue on his or her Life Path. Positive Beings are in control of their destiny and timeline. They feel good about who they are becoming in life. They know the True Self and use their intuition to move forward effortlessly on their path. The ability to know the True Self and live consciously empowers us to make the choices that best meet our goals in life.

Once the Life Path is visible, we can decide if we wish to continue with our current approach or change it to speed up our progress. We only have the ability to change our patterns of approach when we begin living on our Life Path consciously.

We are choosing to walk blindly on our Life Path when we live life unconsciously. If we live life unconsciously, we are choosing to live dangerously. We cannot avoid the potholes in front of us if we do not open our eyes. We also cannot avoid running ourselves off our Life Path if we are driving down it blindly.

The obstacle that many people face today is a lack of intuitive awareness. They ignore the intuitive ability they have to guide themselves forward into the Success State. They do not utilize their voice of intuition to keep them on their Life Path. Instead, they inch themselves along with their intuitive eyes shut tight and then stick their big toe out in front of them until they bump into something. If they open their intuitive eyes at that point, they crash into fear and anxiety. Then they find ways to stop themselves from going forward to avoid running into more fear and anxiety.

Yet, the universe is always at work for us. It constantly nudges us forward if we become stuck. Like the branch that gets lodged on the edge of a river bank, the tides of the universe are always flowing around us. For those of us who allow the universe to work with us, we find a force moving us back into the flow of the current. It is like having our sails up waiting for the gentle winds to gather in them and move us forward without much effort on our part. The winds do all the work for us. If our sails are down, the flow of the winds will move through the masts without us and leave us standing still.

It is up to us to decide whether we want to work with the natural rhythm and flow of the universe. Just like the branch that is lodged on the edge of the river bank, the same current that pushed it out to the edge will eventually pass by to draw it back into the flow of the river again. This is also how the universe guides us through life to our destiny. No matter how much we resist, the tides of the universe are a greater force than we are individually. The question is, how much of ourselves are we going to let erode away in our resistance?

We cannot find out our starting Point A when we do not know the True Self. It does not matter how much time or effort we spend looking for our Destiny or Life's Purpose, we will live unconsciously until we know the True Self. If we cannot consciously connect the True Self with our Destiny, then our path remains *invisible* to our conscious mind. We continue moving forward, stumbling around and sometimes hurting ourselves needlessly in this blindness. We constantly have that "lost feeling" in the pit of our stomach. We dwell on hope and lose it quickly when the smallest of obstacles comes our way. But when we live consciously, our intuition tells us how to move about safely if we fall into the darkness. For example, our intuition can give us encouragement by telling us how long it will take to pass through a difficult situation keeping us motivated when life gets tough.

The fastest way to find your Destiny is to find your Life's Purpose. Once you see your direction in life, you start to see the markers that are there to guide you toward your Destiny. The ability to see your progress keeps you moving forward. You can reach your Destiny when you are living life at your full potential. You are only cheating yourself when you hold yourself back. The reason why does not matter.

Finding your Life's Purpose is a journey into the self through the subconscious mind. The subconscious mind speaks to us loudest when we are dreaming. While we are awake, the conscious mind is active in the driver's seat and the subconscious mind rides in the passenger seat. It lets the conscious mind do all the driving.

The subconscious mind works with our intuitive voice. Together, the subconscious mind and intuition send messages through the body. When our subconscious mind and intuition communicate with our consciousness, they express their messages loudest when they are blocked. Illness and injury are two ways that our subconscious mind speaks to us through the body. Even though we call mishaps, "accidents," the savvy Success State warriors realize that there are no "accidents" in the universe, only lessons that we learn.

How do you know when you are living in the Success State? What are the sign posts? First of all, you will relinquish your will to the unknown. You live every day in a state of observance rather than conscious control. Most people would feel out of control if they did not have a schedule for the week already planned. But the Success State achiever does not need one. These people have an internal barometer that tells them how to be in the right place at the right time before they consciously know why. Sometimes Success State achievers try to book appointments and cannot do it because their intuition tells them to hold off. This is because there is an event manifesting that has not been created yet. If they override their intuitive feelings and book the appointment anyway, when the opportunity finally manifests as an unexpected windfall opportunity, they will not be available to take advantage of it.

We do not have to repeat our life lessons when we glean what we need to know to move forward. We will be periodically tested to make sure we do not slide backward. We acquire the wisdom to avoid similar circumstances when we appreciate the choices we make. That is when personal choice is activated and personal power is wielded. When we can joust with candor and stay seated in the presence of our challenges, we advance on the path toward our Destiny. We live in the Success State when we move toward our destiny at our full potential.

The Last Four Steps to achieving Success State Living are:

4. Finding Your Life Path
5. Learning to Follow Your Life Path
6. Becoming Your Life Path
7. Moving Beyond Your Life Path

When you are ready to find your Life Path, you need to have the ability to cope with the truth your intuition shows you. The reason many people refuse to listen to their intuition is they do not know how to cope with the truth. It is virtually impossible to find your Life Path if you are unwilling to accept the truth. Remember, there is no starting Point A if we do not know the True Self. The path will remain invisible to us until we consciously begin our journey. We can live unconsciously and wander around indefinitely thorough our life without direction. But we give up so much of our personal power and time when we live unconsciously.

When you are pursuing the task of finding your path, you must remember that intuition is your most potent guide. As you hear the truth, you will increase your coping skills as you blast through the illusions and face reality. Then you can begin to create a trusting relationship with your body and intuition. Your physical body teaches you to speak clearly. Are you creating good health (balance), illness (imbalance), or disease (dropping your defenses)? You will always know what you are creating when you listen to your body. As you struggle to create the trust in your relationship with your intuition, you build the vocabulary the body will use to communicate with you.

The more you listen to your intuition, the more it will speak to you. As with any relationship, the more you share with each other, the more you trust the other. When you finally trust your intuition, it will show you your Life's Path. The important thing to know is your intuition knows the *exact* moment you are ready.

It is not enough to just find your Life Path. You must learn to follow it. Listening to your intuition is also not enough. Your intuition is a truth-bearer. It is a messenger, but not a decision-maker. It will tell you the truth, but *you* will decide what to do with that truth. Some people will deny it and some people will block it. Success State people utilize the truth to maximize their potential and make the most of the choices that yield the greatest rewards. They embrace the opportunities and don't waste time in indecision. They learn how to use what they know to climb upward on their Life Path. They do not need proof to support what their intuition tells them so they do not waste time looking for answers to things they already know. Their intuition saves them time and suffering by jumping them ahead of those who do not trust their intuition.

When you are learning to follow your Life Path, you will have experiences both on and off your path so that you can learn how to differentiate between the two experiences. There is no other way for you to learn this skill, so accept that it is a natural part of your learning curve during this part of your journey. Some people expect their path to be pain free, but this is a mistake that can send you off your path. Part of the life journey is to learn how to cope with new and different situations. This stretches your repertoire of skills along your path. Once you learn the basics, you can safely speed up and shorten the time and distance to living in your Success State. Learning how to tackle the curves on the path without falling off will move you on to greater responsibility and peace of mind.

Intuition is a major factor in Success State achievers. You automatically live in the Success State every moment of your life without consciously trying when you achieve the ultimate platform of love for the self. How you approach your life in the Success State is far different than the approach of the intellectual mind. The key to maintaining the Success State is shifting from living in the conscious mind to living in love for the Infinite Self through the subconscious. This shift is the most important one a Success State person can make in his or her life.

When you become your Life Path, you merge with your True Self, your Destiny, and your Life's Purpose. You begin to manifest what you need to experience in life to reach your full potential at a subconscious level. Responsibility for the outcomes is essential. Awareness of what you are manifesting is important to the creation of your Life Path. Life is in its fullest bloom when you become your Life Path. The flowers of love and laughter are more palpable and their fragrance is much more intense. When you can accept the truth, you see life from a whole new perspective. Everything you see in life is more vibrant and alive before you become your path. It's like watching a black and white movie and then seeing it again in color. There is no comparison in the experience of the colorized version. It's incredible!

When you become your Life Path, you can see relationships *before* they come into fruition. This means you can manifest something different before it happens in the physical realm. For example, if you see a storm heading toward you in the distance, you can change your course *before* it hits. Or, you can take a rain jacket, umbrella, and boots to protect yourself from the storm that is coming. You have extra time to prepare or make other arrangements. When you are the captain of your own destiny you become your Life Path. You choose the outcomes that you desire. The more you can do for yourself, the more you appreciate the rewards and pitfalls that you create in your life.

The experience for the artist is much different than it is for its audience. The power to choose the color palate and medium, etc. belongs solely to the active role of the artist. The audience experiences the work of the artist. Their participation is a passive role dependent on what the artist chooses to create.

If we look at children when they first begin to draw, they start out drawing basic shapes and stick figures. They learn to process what they see onto paper with crayons. They learn a variety of skills to produce the outcomes they desire. If they receive the support and encouragement they need, they will continue to move forward in learning to draw. They begin to explore new concepts and eventually master the craft.

Learning to create in a supportive environment can have an enormous impact on the progress of a new skill. There are also many internal factors that can affect the pursuit of a new skill like personality, motivation, and talent to name a few. Perseverance and patience are crucial in how we *cope* with what we produce in the learning stages.

If we do not accept what we create when we are learning to manifest, then we will end up like the artist who shreds his or her first several works of art. Many artists put themselves in a tirade of anger and self-hatred because of imperfections in the work they produced in the learning stages. If they allow their self-hatred and punishment to continue, they will destroy themselves by manifesting one nightmarish disaster after another. Or they will finally learn to accept their new manifesting skills to create a beautiful Life Path to fulfill their Destiny and Life's Purpose.

The key to becoming your Life Path is to be able to *accept* your imperfect attempts when you are first learning to manifest. This acceptance is crucial to moving forward on the Life Path that you are learning to create. Your progress will continue to move you forward on your journey or it will cease altogether if you become distressed by your creations. If you jump off your path completely, you will need to begin all over again and you will not achieve your destiny.

Once we have mastered our inner abilities of acceptance and responsibility, we can begin to create the life our conscious mind desires. It is important to keep an awareness of *why* we are manifesting. Are we manifesting the things that we need to reach our destiny or are we losing touch with what we are trying to accomplish in our life's purpose? This is the constant challenge that we face each time we begin the creative process in becoming our Life Path.

We are in touch with the spiritual self when we become our Life Path. No matter what we call it, we have accessed the God within us. This is the source of our manifesting powers. When we contact the God force within us and bring it to the physical world that we live in, we begin to produce what we are carrying in our subconscious mind.

Whether we are aware of our subconscious thought or not, we manifest on the subconscious level. This is why accurate dream analysis is so essential to our manifesting on a moment-to-moment basis. We are what we dream! If we are living in a subconscious state of fear, then we will manifest some big nightmares. The blessing in the manifesting process is that all creations are manifested out of love. Whether it is out of love for the self or out of love of fear, we will eventually show ourselves what exists in our subconscious mind. When we know what exists in our subconscious mind, we can change it.

We are able to understand why the others around us have the same mindset as we do in the subconscious mind when we can accept the True Self. Whether it is in health or finance, anger or doubt, there is a common subconscious factor involved. Each one of us has the choice to let go of the feelings or thought processes that are plaguing us at the time. When we are filled with love, joy, and peace of mind from the spirit, protection from the nightmares within becomes unnecessary. Learning to access them at will is an important part of maintaining ourselves in the Success State.

What we do with our lives and our own personal evolution is by choice. There are no accidents in this lifetime, only the choices that we create. We are ready to move beyond our Life Path into the realm of all possibilities when we can accept the responsibility of what we are choosing. It is here in the place beyond the Life Path that we converge with the God within and become the mighty beings that we were meant to be in this lifetime. This is the full potential that every living being can become in life. Living in the Success State brings us closer to our full potential, but it is only when we move beyond our Life Path that we become our Infinite Self. Letting go of the self completely is the only way to be the Infinite Self.

You will find the beginning of the life you really want to live when you move to the place where the logical mind cannot follow. This is the place where pain and suffering cannot survive. This guards the entryway to the Infinite Self. This is where you leave behind the trivia that bogs down the logical mind with questions during your assent into deep meditation. When you release your pain and suffering without guilt, you reach the place where you manifest the answers to your deepest prayers in the Infinite Self. This is the place that can be accessed at anytime, and once reached it connects you to the Infinite Creative Source within you.

The most important part of your dreams is communication from the Infinite Self to your subconscious. The subconscious mind cannot always communicate what it knows with the conscious mind because of the personality. The personality varies with every lifetime, but it can be disengaged from the conscious mind when we sleep. During the sleep process, we let our mind and body release burdens. This is why we need so much sleep when we are stressed.

You will find a happy place to rest in between the realms while entering the meditative state. Relax and find yourself drifting to that place you need to address before moving on into the invisible realms of infinite composition and utmost pleasure in solitude. You will find the best times of your life in these invisible realms of plenitude and joy. The euphoric exhilaration of the Infinite Self is beyond verbal description. The elimination of the need to describe the experience opens the gateway to being in the creative state, and knowingness is the password and security against the doubt that bars non-believers from this reality.

You know you are maintaining yourself in the Success State when you can unequivocally make your most important life decisions based on your intuition and not your logical mind. There is no way for intellectual decision-makers to compete with Success State decision-makers who are manifesting their destiny with their intuitive mind. The intuitive Success State achievers are receiving their guidance from their creative intuitive forces that are manifesting their Life Path toward their Life's Purpose and Destiny. Intellectual decision-makers are making their decisions based on the limited capacities of their logical mind. The intellectual approach has more to do with the ego than the decision-maker's Destiny or life's purpose.

You can begin anytime in this lifetime when you are ready to enter this arena of utter creation. There are no financial minimums to be met nor is there any social status or intellectual achievement barriers. There is only the minimum of the internal spiritual secrets that prayer and meditation provide for us in their solitude. You will enter the world of the Infinite Self at the most unexpected time. You cannot anticipate your entry in any lifetime because it occurs spontaneously. So, be at peace with its entry and you will be sure to arrive on time.

Judith Shinoda Berry, MBA

JUDITH SHINODA BERRY, MBA is an international speaker, action success coach, and highly sought-after educator in the field of Business Intuition. She helps business executives, entrepreneurs, sales representatives, and others learn that professional success is a reflection of their own personal healing and transformation.

Judith is a charismatic, compelling speaker and a powerful motivating presence. She has been seen on numerous television shows such as *Bridging Heaven and Earth, The Optimal Health, Optimal Wealth Show, The Next Step, Spectrum Television,* and more as she guides audiences to new heights of intuitive insight and growth. She conducts seminars and retreats globally in intuitive development, application, technology, and advancement.

Judith Shinoda Berry, MBA
Phone: 805.654.9498
E-mail: info@judithshinoda.com
www.judithshinoda.com